COLIN FASSNIDGE knows good food. As a celebrated chef and popular television personality, he has built his reputation on delicious food and his distinctive, no-nonsense advice for home cooks.

When it comes to cooking at home, Colin believes it comes down to common sense. Master the basics – a simple omelette, a great sauce that goes with everything, the perfect roast – and you have the foundations for countless meals. Embrace cheaper cuts of meat, minimise waste, keep a good stock of pantry staples and, whatever you do, don't throw out those delicious parmesan rinds!

Leftovers can be a thing of beauty, too: roast a show-stopping whole cauliflower and turn the leftovers into a miso-based soup; a beef cheek pie filling doubles as a delicious pasta sauce. Sweet indulgences are endlessly adaptable: choose your own ice-cream adventure with the perfect base for many flavours; make a tarte tatin, clafoutis or summer jelly recipe your own by using your family's favourite seasonal fruit.

THIS IS REAL FAMILY FOOD MADE EASY.

This is dedicated to the women in my house.
You made me fall in love with food again.

The COMMONSENSE COOK

COLIN FASSNIDGE

plum. Pan Macmillan Australia

CONTENTS

INTRODUCTION

Growing up in an Irish household, everything was about food and the dining-room table was the focus of family life. It was the central point for daily to-dos, school reports, arguments and heated discussions about politics and religion. Of course, whenever sex was brought up in conversation, my mother quickly left the table! Ultimately, in our household, food was an ongoing display of love throughout the day. Both my parents cooked, and it was pretty early on that I knew I wanted to be a chef. During a time I refer to as the 'Billy Elliot era', being a chef was not seen as a masculine job. But both my parents said to me, 'If you're going to do it, go cook for the best in the world'.

Cooking in my early years was all about cooking for love. There are some dishes and aromas that still take me back to an exact time and place in my life, the way that only food can do. These moments were the foundations of my cooking career. As time goes by, when a young punk chef enters the high-end kitchens, it's more about precision and art – the love can get a little lost. But it's essential to go through all that to get back to the roots of where you started from.

In my youth of excess, I used to knock all the old chefs who said 'less is more!' ... and now I am one of those old guys. They were right, though – less really *is* more. An old saying thrown around when I was a young gun was to let the ingredients speak for themselves. But a young chef always wants to go one step further to prove skill, genius ... and ego. As experience takes over, it becomes important to know your producers, know the provenance. Knowing where your food comes from evokes a sense of belonging – the food to the place, and a memory to the food. Good dishes are the ones that make you stop and reflect, taking you back to the first time you smelled it, saw it, tasted it. Delving into nostalgia, taste can transport you back decades; skill is about bringing that to the plate. By cooking – and sharing – these dishes, you're now imparting these memories to the next generation. The Italians have done this for years ... now the Irish are taking up the baton!

THE NEXT ROUND

This is the cookbook I've always wanted to write but was never brave enough to. You know, the type of bravery that comes with age and grey hair.

Back when I wrote my first cookbook, I was still deep in the world of restaurants and the hectic pace that goes with it. Add to that the glitz and glamour of being a newfound television star (you're welcome), juggling my time between the television kitchen, my restaurant kitchen and my home kitchen, I found myself running at a million miles an hour. Don't get me wrong, I love that kind of energy, but there's a lot to be said for stopping for a second to enjoy the moment. Since then, a lot has changed in my life – I've slowed down, and I've rediscovered the joy in cooking food that simply makes me happy.

Now, a few years later, out of the restaurant grind and cooking much simpler food, I'm remembering the essence of what I actually love. For me, slowing down the pace of life means more cooking at home with friends and family, over coal fires and barbecues, with stories and red wine. I'm now able to cook the food I love to eat and the food I love to share. I started to note down the meals that put a smile on people's faces and stuck those recipes on a wall. Even my kids, Lily and Maeve, started sticking their favourite recipes up to remind me which ones to cook again, each recipe (sometimes brutally) rated by them.

It was during this process that I realised I had nothing to prove anymore. I'm now old and battle-wise and I'm just cooking the food I started out with as a kid – achievable food that warms the heart and makes people happy.

THE COMMONSENSE COOK

It has taken my own personal growth and 20 years of development as a chef to bring me to a place where I realise what's important about food, and what I want to teach and share with people. So many people tell me they can't cook and I just don't believe this is true. I want you to realise that you CAN cook; all you need is a good grounding in the basics and some commonsense kitchen know-how to develop a repertoire of family favourites. (And this book, course.)

First of all, and probably most importantly, don't be afraid of cooking. Professional kitchens can create food fear and the need for food to be Instagram-ready. The dishes in this book have all come through the love of good produce, not fear. Bringing enjoyment to family and friends through food is the most important thing you can do with your cooking. So, do that.

Also, keep it approachable. Creating comfort food is all about the dishes that are close to your heart, those that put a smile on your face and make you feel happy, loved, safe and secure. The recipes in this book are inspired by everything from childhood memories to the changing of the seasons, and take into account the guilty pleasures and sweet indulgences that everyone enjoys.

I've added little notes about waste, and almost every dish in this book has two uses. Sometimes the second night's dish is even better than the first. In saying this, you should know that not all of these dishes worked the first time round in my house – three women can be tough judges – but the recipes have since been fixed, gone through the family test again, and finally approved.

Sometimes it feels like we all take cooking a little too seriously, making it a lot harder than it needs to be. Cooking should, above all, be fun and taste good. Comfort cooking is exactly that – it demands you strip back all fanfare and cook the food you'd make and eat with family and friends. So, with this book, I wanted to make cooking easy again, to share recipes and commonsense techniques that empower people to get back in the kitchen, to take away the fear and bring back the fun of cooking. And, of course, to pass down these recipes as my parents did to me.

This book was finished amidst COVID-19, the crisis management of which has been a difficult adjustment for many all around the world. However, one positive to emerge during the ordeal is families being brought back home around the table, encouraging family cooking, togetherness, teaching, growing and eating new things. I want the recipes in this book to be cooked at family tables and passed on, so that in later years kids will cook them at their own family dinners, reminding them of childhood meals just as many of these dishes bring back memories of my growing up in Dublin as a young boy.

Most importantly, this is a book for every occasion – the simple lunch, a family dinner or that special event. It will help you master the basics and therefore give you the foundations for countless delicious and achievable meals. It will give you the confidence to embrace cheaper or different cuts of meat, get creative with leftovers and apply commonsense in the kitchen to your great advantage. I want the food in this book to be stress free and enjoyed and tweaked by you to become your family's favourite. Ultimately, I would like this book to sit on your kitchen bench with pages stained, marked and worn from use. And maybe it'll get you started on your own family recipe wall.

A good salad is all about great produce and a killer dressing. See page 21 for my family's favourite!

SALADS

WATERMELON, FENNEL, PEA AND FETA SALAD

SERVES 6

I love to serve this refreshing summer salad with the sticky pork ribs on page 146 or my lamb on a brick on page 179, as the watermelon perfectly cuts through the richness of the meat. Serving the salad in the carved-out watermelon is a great trick that never fails to impress. You can even eat the 'bowl'!

½ small watermelon
2 fennel bulbs, finely sliced, fronds reserved
200 g thawed frozen peas
½ bunch of mint, leaves picked
200 ml extra-virgin olive oil
zest and juice of 2 lemons
sea salt and freshly ground black pepper
200 g feta

Using a large metal spoon, scoop the flesh out of the watermelon and chop it into bite-sized chunks.

Using a large sharp knife, slice the bottom off the hollowed-out watermelon, without cutting all the way through, to create a flat base. This will be your salad bowl.

Combine the sliced fennel bulb, peas, mint, olive oil, lemon zest and juice in a large bowl and season with salt and pepper. Crumble over the feta and mix through using your hands. Taste and adjust the seasoning if necessary.

Gently toss the chopped watermelon through the salad, then transfer to the melon bowl and serve with a scattering of fennel fronds.

TIP!

You can also use rockmelon instead of watermelon and add sliced parma ham to the salad bowl at the end.

SPROUT SLAW

SERVES 4-6

This light interpretation of the classic slaw celebrates that much underrated vegetable – the brussels sprout – and with a fraction of the mayonnaise you could almost call it healthy!

6 bacon rashers
300 g brussels sprouts, trimmed
50 g capers, rinsed and drained, chopped
50 g cornichons, rinsed and drained, chopped
3 teaspoons whole-egg mayonnaise
1 tablespoon dijon mustard
bunch of flat-leaf parsley, leaves picked and chopped
2 tablespoons sherry vinegar
sea salt and freshly ground black pepper
50 g roasted hazelnuts, skins removed, chopped

Preheat the oven grill to high.

Place the bacon under the grill and cook for 5–7 minutes, until crisp. Roughly chop.

Cut the sprouts in half and finely slice on a mandoline into a bowl. Add the bacon, capers and cornichons and give everything a good stir.

Mix through the mayonnaise and mustard until the ingredients are well coated, then add the parsley, vinegar and salt and pepper to taste. Combine thoroughly, transfer to a serving plate and sprinkle over the hazelnuts. Serve with your choice of grilled meat.

CELERY SALAD WITH VIERGE DRESSING

SERVES 4

Celery may not be the cure-all touted by social media influencers, but it is certainly delicious. This humble veg adds incredible crunch and texture to dishes, but in this simple salad I've made it the star of its own show.

½ bunch of celery
100 g toasted pine nuts
200 ml Vierge Dressing
　　(see page 21)
sea salt and freshly ground
　　black pepper

Slice each celery stalk into thirds lengthways, then finely slice across. Set aside the celery leaves.

Place the sliced celery and pine nuts in a bowl and toss through the vierge dressing. Check the seasoning and adjust if necessary, then spoon the mixture onto a serving plate. Top with the reserved celery leaves and serve.

For a twist, scatter over some shaved pecorino, along with the celery leaves.

SPICED BROCCOLINI AND MARLON'S CHEESE SALAD

SERVES 4

My good friend Marlon Dalton showed me this quick recipe for fresh cheese about 10 years ago. I thought it ingenious at the time, and have been using it ever since. It's so simple and versatile, and pairs wonderfully with broccolini for a light lunch or side dish.

2½ tablespoons sesame oil
1 tablespoon red wine vinegar
2 teaspoons chilli flakes
100 g cashew nuts, toasted and
    roughly chopped
2 tablespoons sesame seeds, toasted
sea salt and freshly ground
    black pepper
2 bunches of broccolini

MARLON'S EASY CHEESE
2 x 600 ml cartons buttermilk
juice of 2 lemons
200 ml olive oil
sea salt
100 g fennel seeds, finely crushed
    to a powder

To make Marlon's easy cheese, fill a large saucepan two-thirds full with water and lower in the unopened cartons of buttermilk. Bring to a simmer over medium heat and cook for 45 minutes.

Allow the cartons to cool slightly, then open them up and tip the contents into a large square of muslin. Tie the corners of the muslin together to make a bag, then hang the bag over a bowl or jug to collect the whey that drains off (see the Tip below for what to do with this). Set aside in the fridge for 6 hours.

Place the buttermilk curds that have collected in the muslin in the bowl of a food processor and add the lemon juice and olive oil. Season with salt and blend to a smooth consistency. Add the powdered fennel seeds and season to taste, then blend again until completely smooth.

Store the cheese in an airtight container in the fridge for up to 1 week.

Combine the sesame oil, red wine vinegar, chilli flakes, cashews and sesame seeds in a large bowl. Season to taste with salt and pepper and set aside.

Bring a saucepan of salted water to the boil over medium heat, add the broccolini and blanch for 3 minutes until al dente – don't overcook it! Drain well, shaking off any excess water, then toss the hot broccolini through the dressing.

Spoon the cheese onto a serving plate and arrange the broccolini over the top. Serve warm.

You can make a salad dressing from the leftover whey. Just mix it with some extra-virgin olive oil and a splash of lemon juice.

A SIMPLE GREEN SALAD WITH VIERGE DRESSING

SERVES 4

A simple green salad should be in everyone's repertoire. I use this recipe as a starting point and then swap out the leaves and herbs for whatever is currently growing in our garden. The French vierge dressing is great served with your favourite meat and fish dishes or used as a salad dressing as I've done here. The dressing will keep in the fridge for up to 2 weeks – just shake well before using. You'll need to make it the day before you want to use it.

100 g rocket

4 Tuscan kale leaves, leaves torn, stalks finely sliced

4 rainbow silverbeet leaves, leaves torn, stalks finely sliced

½ bunch of basil, leaves picked and torn

2 tarragon sprigs, leaves picked and torn

2 marjoram sprigs, leaves picked and torn

extra-virgin olive oil or hemp oil, for drizzling

VIERGE DRESSING (MAKES 1 LITRE)

100 g coriander seeds, toasted

2 star anise, toasted

1 litre extra-virgin olive oil

3 bunches of basil, leaves picked

½ bunch of mint, leaves picked

½ bunch of flat-leaf parsley, leaves picked

sea salt and freshly ground black pepper

freshly squeezed lemon juice, to taste

For the vierge dressing, place the coriander seeds, star anise, olive oil and herbs in a blender and blend until smooth. Don't over-blend the ingredients as you want to avoid the heat of the blender warming the dressing. Transfer the dressing to a bowl and season to taste with salt and pepper. Cover and set aside in the fridge for 24 hours for the flavours to infuse.

The next day, strain the dressing through a fine sieve and transfer to an airtight bottle or jar. Before using, season to taste with salt and lemon juice.

For the salad, combine the rocket, kale, silverbeet and herbs in a salad bowl and mix well using your hands.

Spoon over enough vierge dressing to lightly coat the leaves and toss to combine.

Drizzle with olive oil or hemp oil and serve immediately.

Lily & Maeve's Tip

Eat your greens. Our mum said!

RAW ASPARAGUS, BABY COS AND HAZELNUT SALAD

SERVES 4

When in season, asparagus is on high rotation in my kitchen. There's no need to cook the asparagus in this salad – the raw stems taste lovely and sweet on their own as well as providing a fresh crunch.

2 bunches of asparagus,
   woody ends removed
4 radishes
2 baby cos lettuce, leaves
   roughly torn
100 g roasted hazelnuts, skins
   removed, roughly chopped
2½ tablespoons extra-virgin olive oil
2½ tablespoons hazelnut oil
3 teaspoons freshly squeezed
   lemon juice
3 teaspoons white wine vinegar
1 teaspoon caster sugar
sea salt and freshly ground
   black pepper

Using a vegetable peeler, shave the asparagus into long lengths to look like noodles. Shave the radishes into thin discs.

Combine the cos lettuce leaves, asparagus noodles, radish and hazelnuts in a salad bowl.

In a separate bowl, whisk together the olive and hazelnut oils, lemon juice, vinegar and sugar. Season to taste with salt and pepper, then toss through the salad.

Serve immediately.

SHAVED RAW BEETROOT SALAD WITH HORSERADISH AND MASH MAYONNAISE

SERVES 4

Raw beetroot is earthy, crunchy and sweet all at the same time, and when paired with one of my favourite ingredients, fresh horseradish, this much-loved vegetable takes on a whole new dimension. If you can, seek out different varieties of beetroot for this salad: I like target, red and golden as their colours really pop off the plate. This is a great way to use up leftover mashed potato.

½ fresh horseradish root, peeled
    and grated
100 ml olive oil
10 heirloom baby beetroot bulbs,
    stalks attached, scrubbed clean
200 g cold mashed potato
    (see page 71)
100 g whole-egg mayonnaise
juice of ½ lemon
1 tablespoon dijon mustard
1 tablespoon capers, rinsed and
    drained, chopped
50 g cornichons, rinsed and drained,
    finely chopped
sea salt and freshly ground
    black pepper
1 tablespoon apple cider vinegar

Combine the horseradish and olive oil in a large bowl and set aside.

Using a mandoline, finely shave the beetroot bulbs, then finely slice the stalks with a knife. Place the beetroot on a plate, cover with a damp cloth so it doesn't dry out and set aside in the fridge.

Combine the mashed potato, mayonnaise, lemon juice, mustard, capers and cornichons in a bowl and season to taste with salt and pepper.

Spread the potato mixture over a large serving plate.

Add the vinegar to the horseradish oil, then toss through the shaved beetroot bulbs and stalks.

Arrange the beetroot over the potato mixture and serve with a little horseradish dressing drizzled over the top.

CABBAGE AND FENNEL SLAW

SERVES 6–8

Crunch and texture. Texture and crunch ... A good slaw is a fantastic and simple way to give yourself a vegetable boost. You can pair a slaw with pretty much anything, but my personal favourite has to be a good chicken schnitzel (see page 118). In this recipe, I've included fennel and silverbeet for a twist on the classic cabbage slaw.

6 silverbeet leaves, finely chopped
200 g red cabbage, finely sliced
2 red onions, finely sliced
1 fennel bulb, trimmed and finely
   sliced from top to bottom
bunch of flat-leaf parsley, leaves and
   stalks roughly chopped
300 g whole-egg mayonnaise,
   plus extra if needed
juice of 1 lemon
sea salt and freshly ground
   black pepper
extra-virgin olive oil, for drizzling

Combine the silverbeet, cabbage, onion, fennel and parsley in a large mixing bowl.

Stir through the mayonnaise, adding a little more if you prefer a wetter consistency.

Transfer the slaw to a serving bowl. Add the lemon juice, season well with salt and pepper and drizzle over a little olive oil.

HERBY POTATO SALAD

SERVES 4–6

Most families have a go-to potato salad recipe, and here is mine. Kipflers are one of my all-time favourite potatoes. They're firm and nutty with a great mouthfeel, making them the perfect spud to use in a potato salad. This salad is best served warm.

400 g kipfler potatoes (try to find potatoes that are a similar size and thickness)
sea salt
2 tablespoons capers, rinsed and drained, chopped
12 large pickled white anchovy fillets, chopped
½ bunch of thyme, leaves picked
½ bunch of tarragon, leaves picked
bunch of flat-leaf parsley, leaves picked and roughly chopped
bunch of chives, snipped
juice of 2 lemons
100 ml extra-virgin olive oil
2 tablespoons apple cider vinegar

Place the potatoes in a large saucepan and cover with cold water. Season with salt, then bring to the boil over medium–high heat. Reduce the heat to a simmer and cook the potatoes for 10 minutes or until a knife just slides through the flesh. Don't overcook them – no one likes mushy potato salad! Drain and set aside for 10 minutes, then use a knife to scrape off the skins. Chop the potatoes into large chunks.

Combine the capers, anchovy, herbs, lemon juice, olive oil and apple cider vinegar in a large salad bowl. Toss through the warm potato chunks (their warmth will help absorb the flavour of the dressing) and serve while still warm.

COLLETTE'S BLOOD ORANGE, SWEETCORN AND POMEGRANATE RICE SALAD

SERVES 6

This dish takes me back to childhood picnics in Dublin's Phoenix Park. Mum would always bring along this salad to keep us kids happy. Of course, the chef in me has jazzed it up with the addition of pomegranate seeds and vierge dressing; just don't tell Collette!

6 sweetcorn cobs, husks and
  silks removed
500 g cooked white rice, chilled
6 blood oranges (or regular oranges
  or mandarins)
seeds of 4 pomegranates
bunch of mint, leaves picked and
  roughly chopped
bunch of flat-leaf parsley, leaves
  picked and roughly chopped
100 ml Vierge Dressing
  (see page 21)
sea salt and freshly ground
  black pepper

Preheat a barbecue grill to high or place a chargrill pan over medium—high heat. Add the corn cobs and cook for about 10 minutes, until nicely charred on all sides. Remove the corn from the grill or pan and, when cool enough to handle, strip the kernels from the cobs. Set the corn aside in a bowl and discard the cobs.

Place the chilled cooked rice in a large mixing bowl and zest over the blood oranges. Peel the zested oranges, then, using a sharp knife, segment the oranges over the rice, allowing the juice to collect in the bowl and adding the segments as you go.

Stir through the pomegranate seeds and reserved corn, along with the herbs. Toss through the vierge dressing and season with salt and pepper.

Transfer to a serving bowl and serve.

VEGETABLES

From tarts and turnovers to the perfect potato mash, my veggie section has you covered for any occasion.

A GREEN SAUCE TO GO WITH EVERYTHING

MAKES 500 ML (2 CUPS)

I first created this sauce after we ended up with an excess of leafy greens in our veggie patch the first year. It's now a staple in our household. What I love most about this sauce is that you never get the exact same flavour two times in a row, as it all depends on the variety and abundance of each leaf type. As the title suggests, serve this sauce with anything and everything to add a hit of freshness to your dishes.

2 bunches of leafy greens,
    such as silverbeet, kale, sorrel
    or whatever is in season, leaves
    and stalks roughly chopped
4 bird's eye chillies, roughly chopped
2 makrut lime leaves
50 g ginger, roughly chopped
300 ml extra-virgin olive oil
2 heaped teaspoons dijon mustard
250 ml (1 cup) white wine vinegar
1 tablespoon fish sauce
soy sauce, to season

Place all the ingredients except the soy sauce in the bowl of a food processor and blitz until you have a smooth, bright green sauce. Season to taste with soy sauce.

Use immediately or store in an airtight container in the fridge for up to 2 weeks.

SERVE ME WITH

GRILLED MEAT
OR COLD CUTS
(SEE PAGE 171).

CHANGE UP THE GREENS
ACCORDING TO THE
SEASON SO YOU GET
TO TASTE THEM ALL.

TOSS ME THROUGH
LEFTOVER ROAST MEAT
AND VEGGIES FOR
A HEARTY SALAD
(SEE PAGE 141).

The only thing
this doesn't go with
is dessert!

SIMPLE SWEETCORN AND BACON FRITTERS

SERVES 6

Breakfast, brunch or lunch; it doesn't really matter what time of day you make these delicious fritters. Served with creme fraiche on the side, it only takes a few minutes to put together restaurant-quality fritters without needing to leave the house.

4 streaky bacon rashers,
    roughly chopped
50 g (⅓ cup) plain flour
2 teaspoons baking powder
125 ml (½ cup) full-cream milk
2 large eggs, separated
4 spring onions, finely chopped
1 sweetcorn cob, husks and silks
    removed, kernels stripped
1 bird's eye chilli, finely chopped
2–3 tablespoons extra-virgin olive oil
sea salt and freshly ground
    black pepper
creme fraiche, to serve

Heat a small frying pan over medium heat, add the streaky bacon and fry for 2–3 minutes, until crisp. Set aside to cool.

Combine the flour and baking powder in the bowl of a stand mixer with the whisk attached. Slowly whisk in the milk and egg yolks on low speed until you have a smooth batter. Transfer the batter to a large mixing bowl.

Thoroughly clean and dry the bowl of the stand mixer, then tip in the egg whites and whisk on medium speed until soft peaks form.

Fold the crispy bacon, spring onion, sweetcorn and chilli through the batter, then gently fold through the beaten egg white until just combined.

Heat the olive oil in a frying pan over low heat. Working in batches, scoop heaped tablespoons of the sweetcorn and bacon mixture into the pan and cook for 3 minutes on each side or until golden brown. Transfer the fritters to a plate lined with paper towel to drain.

Sprinkle a little salt and pepper over the fritters and serve warm with creme fraiche on the side for dipping.

Lily & Maeve's Tip

The ONLY breakfast Dad does well!

POSH CAULIFLOWER CHEESE

SERVES 4–6

Along with my show-stopping roasted pumpkin (see page 69), I like to serve this whole cauliflower cheese – leaves and all – whenever we serve our whole pig feast at my pubs. It is even more impressive served at home with your favourite roast.

1 whole cauliflower, leaves attached

CHEESE SAUCE
50 g butter
50 g (⅓ cup) plain flour
700 ml full-cream milk
50 g (½ cup) grated parmesan
50 g (½ cup) grated cheddar

To prepare the cauliflower, carefully remove the green leaves, keeping them intact. Trim the base of the cauliflower and discard.

Bring a large saucepan of salted water to the boil over medium–high heat and blanch the green leaves for 1 minute. Using tongs, remove the leaves and refresh them in iced water. Set aside.

Add the whole cauliflower to the boiling water and blanch for 4 minutes or until just cooked, then remove and set aside.

Heat a small frying pan over medium heat and dry off the cauliflower head in the pan for 20 minutes, moving the cauliflower head around to ensure you dry all the florets. Transfer the cauliflower to a small baking dish.

Preheat the oven to 180°C (fan-forced).

To make the cheese sauce, melt the butter in a saucepan over medium heat. Stir in the flour, then reduce the heat to low and cook for 3–4 minutes, until the mixture looks like wet sand. Pour in all the milk at once and whisk constantly to prevent any lumps from forming. Keep stirring until the sauce starts to thicken, then bring the sauce to a simmer and continue to whisk for 5 minutes or until you have a smooth bechamel. Add the grated parmesan and cheddar and whisk until melted. Pour the cheese sauce over the cauliflower and roast in the oven for 30 minutes or until the cheese is golden.

Arrange the green leaves in a serving bowl and place the cheesy whole cauliflower in the middle to make it look like a whole cauliflower again.

LEFTOVERS

Follow the leftovers instructions on page 69 and replace the pumpkin with leftover cauliflower cheese to make a cauliflower and miso soup for lunch the next day.

PEAS, LETTUCE AND PANCETTA

SERVES 4

This light, warm salad is sweet, salty and creamy all at the same time. It's the perfect accompaniment to meals in spring and summer.

2 tablespoons salted butter
1 onion, finely chopped
6 garlic cloves, finely chopped
50 g smoked pancetta, skin
   removed, diced
½ bunch of marjoram, leaves picked
200 g frozen peas, thawed
1 iceberg lettuce, finely sliced
1 radicchio, finely sliced
sea salt and freshly ground
   black pepper
juice of 1 lemon

Melt the butter in a large saucepan over low heat, then add the onion, garlic and pancetta and cook, stirring frequently, for 5 minutes. Add the marjoram and cook for 2 minutes, then stir through the peas until heated through.

Add the lettuce and radicchio and cook, stirring, until the leaves are half wilted. Season with salt and pepper and stir through the lemon juice, then transfer to a serving dish and take to the table.

ROASTED ORANGE AND GARLIC CARROTS

SERVES 6-8

When you slow-roast carrots they become almost meaty. In this recipe, the orange juice reduces down to create a wonderful glossy dressing that coats the carrots. Serve as an accompaniment to the main event or on their own. They're that good!

8–10 large carrots, unpeeled
200 ml extra-virgin olive oil
sea salt and freshly ground
   black pepper
300 ml orange juice
1 garlic bulb, halved horizontally
bunch of thyme
bunch of rosemary
3 star anise
2 cinnamon sticks
1 tablespoon butter

Preheat the oven to 200°C (fan-forced).

Place the carrots in a roasting tin, drizzle over the olive oil and season well with salt and pepper. Roast the carrots, turning occasionally, for 30 minutes or until lightly golden. Pour 200 ml of water into the tin, along with the orange juice, garlic, herbs, star anise, cinnamon sticks and butter. Reduce the temperature to 140°C (fan-forced) and cook for a further 30–40 minutes, until the liquid has reduced by two-thirds and the carrots are completely golden and cooked through.

Transfer the carrots to a serving platter and squeeze over the roasted garlic bulbs. Drizzle with some of the cooking liquid and serve.

GREENS AND RICOTTA TURNOVERS

SERVES 4

A flavoursome vegetable surprise to unwrap. Freeze any leftovers in a zip-lock bag for the perfect time-poor dinner.

100 ml extra-virgin olive oil
2 large red onions, finely sliced
1 fennel bulb, finely sliced
    (slice the fronds and keep
    them for your salad)
sea salt and freshly ground
    black pepper
4 garlic cloves, finely sliced
30 g white anchovy fillets,
    finely chopped
½ bunch of tarragon, leaves picked
    and chopped
½ bunch of sage, leaves picked
    and chopped
1 teaspoon freshly grated nutmeg
1 teaspoon smoked paprika
½ teaspoon chilli flakes
300 g green leaves of your choice,
    such as curly kale, silverbeet or
    sorrel, roughly chopped
2 teaspoons white wine vinegar
300 g full-fat ricotta
4 sheets good-quality frozen
    puff pastry, just thawed
30 g capers, rinsed and drained,
    chopped
small handful of grated parmesan
2 small eggs, beaten
1 tablespoon fennel seeds
½ bunch of thyme, leaves picked
green salad leaves, to serve

HERBED BREADCRUMBS
50 g fresh breadcrumbs
1 rosemary sprig, leaves picked
8 sage leaves
2 thyme sprigs, leaves picked

To make the herbed breadcrumbs, place the ingredients in the small bowl of a food processor and blitz to combine. Set aside.

Heat the olive oil in a frying pan over medium heat. Add the onion, sliced fennel bulb and a good pinch of salt and pepper and cook, stirring constantly, for 15 minutes or until golden brown. Add the garlic and cook for another minute or so, then add the anchovy, herbs, nutmeg, paprika and chilli flakes. Stir to combine, then add your choice of greens and stir through to wilt. Season with a little more salt and pepper, being mindful that the anchovy will have already added quite a bit of salt.

When the greens are wilted, add the vinegar and give everything a stir until combined. Remove from the heat, transfer the mixture to a bowl and chill in the fridge for 45 minutes. Once chilled, stir through the ricotta and then the herbed breadcrumbs – this will help to dry out the mixture.

Place a large baking tray in the oven and preheat it to 180°C (fan-forced).

Lay a puff pastry sheet on your work surface and spread one-quarter of the mixture onto one half of the sheet, leaving a 2 cm border. Scatter over one-quarter of the capers and parmesan. Brush the pastry edges with the beaten egg, then fold the pastry over the filling and trim it into a turnover shape, pinching the edges to seal. Repeat with the remaining pastry and filling to make four turnovers.

Remove the baking tray from the oven and carefully lay a sheet of baking paper on the hot tray. Place the turnovers on the tray and brush with the remaining beaten egg. Sprinkle the fennel seeds, thyme and some salt over the top and grind over some black pepper. Bake for 30 minutes or until the turnovers are puffed up and golden.

Remove the turnovers from the oven and allow to cool. Serve with a fresh garden salad.

MEMORIES OF VINEGAR CHIPS

SERVES 6-8

Our kids love these roast potatoes and they're often top of the list of dishes they ask me to make. The vinegar is a play on chips and malt vinegar – a trend Australia has been missing out on for years. I strongly encourage you to try it!

8–10 desiree potatoes, peeled
   and quartered
sea salt and freshly ground
   black pepper
vegetable oil, for roasting
1 garlic bulb, unpeeled, cloves
   smashed using the side of a knife
bunch of thyme
bunch of rosemary
100 g salted butter, roughly chopped
ROSEMARY VINEGAR
300 ml white wine vinegar
bunch of rosemary, leaves picked
   and chopped
1 tablespoon caster sugar

To make the rosemary vinegar, combine the ingredients in a small bowl and set aside.

Preheat the oven to 200°C (fan-forced).

Place the potato in a large saucepan, cover with cold water and season with salt. Slowly bring to the boil over medium heat, then reduce the heat to a simmer and cook for 20–30 minutes, until the potato is just starting to break up. Drain the potato in a colander and allow to steam dry for about 10 minutes.

While the potato is cooling, pour enough vegetable oil into a roasting tin to cover the base and place it in the oven to heat up. Once the potato is dry, tip it into the roasting tin (be careful as the hot oil will splatter) and spread out in a single layer. Roast for 10 minutes, until the base of each potato is golden brown and crisp. Turn the potato over and add the smashed garlic cloves, herbs and butter. Roast for a further 15 minutes, turning the potato frequently to crisp each side, then remove the tin from the oven and strain away any fat. Season with salt and pepper.

Spoon the rosemary vinegar into the bottom of a serving dish, then gently place the roast potatoes on top and serve.

SWEDE AND CUMIN MASH

SERVES 4–6

A staple of my childhood, swede is a vegetable that has taken me many years to appreciate. Thankfully, I now love this maligned root veg and have learned to cook it in a way that brings out its earthy and sweet flavour. Combined with cumin, this dish makes a great alternative to regular mash.

50 g salted butter
2 red onions, finely sliced
4 garlic cloves, finely chopped
1 parmesan rind
4 swedes, peeled and roughly chopped
1 teaspoon ground cumin
250 ml (1 cup) full-cream milk
250 ml (1 cup) good-quality
   chicken stock
2 bay leaves (fresh if possible)
sea salt and freshly ground
   black pepper
juice of 1 lemon

Melt the butter in a large saucepan over medium heat. Add the onion, garlic and parmesan rind and cook for 5 minutes or until the onion is soft and translucent. Add the swede and cumin and cook for a further 5 minutes, then pour in the milk and stock and stir to combine. Add the bay leaves and season with salt and pepper, then reduce the heat to low and gently cook for about 40 minutes or until the swede is cooked through and completely soft.

Remove the bay leaves and parmesan rind (or leave the rind in if it's completely soft), then gently mash the swede. Add the lemon juice and check the seasoning, adding a little more salt and pepper if needed. Mash again until well combined, then transfer to a dish and serve warm.

TIPS

This recipe works really well with other root vegetables. Check out what's in season and experiment!

For a vegetarian puree, simply replace the chicken stock with a good-quality vegetable stock and seek out a vegetarian parmesan.

SPICY MISO EGGPLANT

SERVES 4–6

Miso and eggplant are a classic pairing in Japan, and in this dish they come together to give umami, spice and sweetness all in one mouthful. The mushrooms add an earthy, 'meaty' texture, making this a great stand-alone dish. Alternatively, share it out and serve with steamed rice.

1 tablespoon sesame oil
1 red onion, finely chopped
20 g ginger, finely chopped
4 garlic cloves, finely sliced
2 long red chillies, finely chopped
2 tablespoons ground coriander
6 king brown mushrooms, diced
2 eggplants
sea salt and freshly ground
   black pepper
30 g sesame seeds, plus extra
   to serve
400 g can diced tomatoes
100 g white miso paste
1 tablespoon vegetable oil
coriander leaves, to serve
1 lime, halved

Preheat the oven to 180°C (fan-forced).

Heat the sesame oil in a frying pan over medium heat. Add the onion, ginger, garlic, chilli, ground coriander and mushroom and cook, stirring frequently, for 20 minutes.

Cut the eggplants in half lengthways and score the flesh in a criss-cross pattern. Sprinkle the cut sides with salt and pepper, then set aside for 10 minutes to allow the salt to penetrate the eggplant.

Add the sesame seeds to the mushroom mixture and cook, stirring, for 4 minutes or until the mushroom is just cooked. Stir through the tomatoes and miso and cook for 10 minutes or until slightly thick and reduced.

Meanwhile, pour the vegetable oil into a roasting tin and place in the oven to heat up. Carefully place the eggplant, cut-side down, in the tin and bake for 6 minutes, then turn the eggplant over and continue to cook for 4 minutes or until the eggplant is just soft.

Remove the eggplant from the oven and carefully pat off any excess oil with paper towel. Using a spoon, gently press into the eggplant flesh to create space for the sauce to sit in.

Spoon the mushroom and tomato mixture onto the eggplant halves, then return to the oven and bake for 20 minutes or until the eggplant is cooked through and the topping has a lovely glaze.

Scatter over some sesame seeds and coriander leaves, squeeze over the lime halves and serve.

ROASTED BEETROOT WITH RED ONION AND GOAT'S CHEESE

SERVES 4–6

This dish is a twist on the classic potato bake. It was the first recipe I tested with the kids for this book, but the only part they liked was the ginger beer! Hasten to say, it was more popular with the adults. Serve this on its own or with a salad for a midweek vegetarian meal.

5 beetroot bulbs, finely sliced
3 red onions, finely sliced into rounds
extra-virgin olive oil, for drizzling
sea salt and freshly ground
    black pepper
½ bunch sage, leaves picked
    and chopped
2 bay leaves (fresh if possible)
pinch of freshly grated nutmeg
100 ml white wine vinegar
200 ml ginger beer
50 g salted butter, chopped
5 cm fresh horseradish root, peeled
150 g goat's cheese
sage leaves, to serve (optional)

Preheat the oven to 180°C (fan-forced).

Place a layer of beetroot and onion overlapping each other in the base of a roasting tin. Drizzle over some extra-virgin olive oil and season with salt and pepper, then scatter over the sage, bay leaves and nutmeg and splash in the vinegar. Layer the remaining beetroot and onion on top. Pour the ginger beer into the tin, then add the butter and push it in between the beetroot and onion. Cover with foil and roast for 40 minutes.

Remove the foil and return the tin to the oven for another 40 minutes (this helps to caramelise the beetroot and reduce the liquid).

Allow the beetroot and onion to a cool little, then transfer to a serving dish. Grate the fresh horseradish over the top and crumble over the goat's cheese. Scatter with sage leaves, if using. Serve warm or cold.

ROASTED SWEET POTATOES WITH SMOKY MAYO

SERVES 6

A salt-baked sweet potato is a thing of beauty. Its flesh is sweet and tender, while the skin is salty, caramelised and chewy. Add a rich, smoky mayo to the mix and you'll take these simple spuds to a whole new level. You might also find yourself with a lot of new friends clamouring for the recipe!

200 g sea salt flakes
6 sweet potatoes
extra-virgin olive oil, to serve
SMOKY MAYO
300 g whole-egg mayonnaise
1 tablespoon smoked paprika
1 teaspoon cayenne pepper
1 teaspoon ground cinnamon
1 teaspoon freshly grated nutmeg
juice of 2 lemons

Preheat the oven to 180°C (fan-forced).

Tip the salt flakes onto a large plate and spread them out. Wash the potatoes and while they are still wet, roll them in the salt flakes.

Place the potatoes directly on an oven shelf and roast for 1 hour or until the skins have crisped up and turned a lovely golden brown and the flesh is cooked through. Set the potatoes aside on a plate and brush away any remaining salt.

Top and tail the potatoes, keeping the ends for the mayonnaise. Halve the potatoes lengthways and place, skin-side up, on a baking tray.

To make the smoky mayo, place the mayonnaise, spices and lemon juice in a blender and blitz to combine. As you blend, add the potato ends and blend until smooth. Transfer the smoky mayo to a serving bowl, cover and place in the fridge until needed.

Preheat the oven grill to high, then grill the sweet potato for 3–4 minutes, keeping a close eye on them to ensure they don't burn, until the skins are blistered. Alternatively, heat a barbecue grill to high or a chargrill pan over high heat and grill the skins on both sides for extra flavour.

Transfer the sweet potato to a serving plate, dollop over the mayonnaise and serve with a drizzle of olive oil.

MY SPICED BREAKFAST OMELETTE

SERVES 3–4

Cooking an omelette is an act of joy that brings together the simplest of ingredients to make a hearty meal. Preparing and cooking this dish always instils in me a sense of calm, allowing me to forget the stresses of the day and focus on making something delicious for family or friends.

6 eggs
1 teaspoon ground coriander
1 teaspoon ground cumin
3 bird's eye chillies, chopped
1 garlic clove, chopped
1 teaspoon finely chopped ginger
bunch of coriander, leaves picked
    and stalks finely chopped
sea salt and freshly ground
    black pepper
2 handfuls of bean sprouts
handful of large-leaf rocket
2 teaspoons fish sauce
1 tablespoon freshly squeezed
    lime juice
½ bunch of mint, leaves picked
20 g roasted peanuts, chopped
1 tablespoon sesame oil

Place the eggs, ground coriander and cumin, two-thirds of the chilli, the garlic, ginger, half the fresh coriander and a pinch of salt and pepper in a blender and blitz until well combined.

Combine the bean sprouts, rocket, fish sauce, lime juice, remaining chilli and fresh coriander, mint and peanuts in a bowl and set aside.

Heat the sesame oil in a large non-stick frying pan over medium heat and pour in the egg mixture. Using a spatula, move the mixture around the pan, pulling the outside into the middle so the mixture cooks evenly. When the bottom of the omelette starts to set, stop mixing with the spatula and leave the omelette to set for 1 minute. Don't overcook the omelette – it should still have a little moisture throughout the egg mixture.

Add the filling to the centre of the omelette and use the spatula to fold the omelette in half over the filling. Slide the omelette onto a serving plate, cut into slices and serve.

POTATO, ONION AND CHEDDAR BAKE

SERVES 6

Potato, onion and cheddar: these are the ingredients I grew up with. Crisp on the outside and gooey in the middle, this is comfort food at its most decadent.

8–10 desiree potatoes, peeled and finely sliced
2 red onions, finely sliced
4 garlic cloves, finely sliced
½ bunch of thyme, leaves picked
200 g grated cheddar
sea salt and freshly ground black pepper
300 ml good-quality chicken stock, heated
extra-virgin olive oil, for drizzling

Preheat the oven to 180°C (fan-forced).

Layer the potato, onion, garlic, thyme, cheese and a little salt and pepper in a large ovenproof frying pan. Pour in the hot chicken stock and cover with foil.

Transfer to the oven and bake for 1 hour, then remove the foil. Return the pan to the oven and cook for 30 minutes or until the top is golden brown and bubbling.

Serve straight away or allow to sit for 30 minutes, then turn out onto a serving plate. Drizzle with olive oil and serve as part of a roast dinner or with a green salad for a hearty supper.

CARAMELISED ONION AND TOMATO TART

SERVES 4

When in season, nothing can beat the intensity or flavour of roasted tomatoes. Here, I pair them with caramelised onions to create an oozy, sticky tart that's perfect for a simple midweek meal.

8 onions, finely sliced
180 ml (¾ cup) extra-virgin olive oil, plus extra for drizzling
bunch of thyme, leaves picked and finely chopped
100 g salted butter
80 ml (⅓ cup) port
80 ml (⅓ cup) apple cider vinegar
sea salt and freshly ground black pepper
1 sheet good-quality frozen puff pastry, just thawed
4 large oxheart tomatoes, sliced in random shapes for texture
1 egg, beaten with a splash of full-cream milk
½ bunch of basil, leaves picked
2 tarragon sprigs, leaves picked

Heat a large saucepan or deep frying pan over high heat. Add the onion, followed by the olive oil and thyme and cook, stirring, for about 4 minutes or until the onion is golden brown. Reduce the heat to low and add the butter. Continue to cook, stirring frequently, for 30 minutes or until the onion is dark brown and caramelised. Add the port and bring to the boil, then stir through the vinegar. Season to taste with salt and pepper and remove from the heat.

Preheat the oven to 200°C (fan-forced).

Place the puff pastry on a baking tray and lightly score the edges of the pastry to create a 1.5 cm border – this allows the edges to rise during cooking. Spread the jammy onion over the pastry within the border, then lay the tomato slices over the top so they overlap each other. Season with salt and pepper, then brush the egg wash over the exposed pastry border.

Transfer to the oven and cook for 35 minutes or until the pastry edges are risen and golden brown, and the tomatoes are caramelised.

Drizzle a little olive oil over the tart and scatter with the basil and tarragon leaves. Divide the tart into quarters and serve with your favourite salad.

TIP

For a twist, place a few blobs of goat's cheese on top of the tomato prior to cooking.

THE SHOW-STOPPER WHOLE ROASTED PUMPKIN

SERVES 4–6

This is a show stopper of a dish that often outshines any meat on the table. The initial high heat and then slow-roasting of the pumpkin softens and caramelises the skin, making it incredibly moreish.

100 ml olive oil
1 x 1 kg whole Japanese pumpkin,
   halved horizontally
sea salt
2 garlic cloves, finely sliced
4 star anise
2 cinnamon sticks, broken up
2 tablespoons fennel seeds
2 tablespoons smoked paprika
¼ bunch of rosemary, roughly chopped
¼ bunch of thyme, roughly chopped
½ bunch of sage, roughly chopped
2 bird's eye chillies, finely chopped
   (optional)
2½ tablespoons sherry vinegar
extra-virgin olive oil, for drizzling

Preheat the oven to 200°C (fan-forced).

Drizzle the olive oil over the cut surface of the pumpkin and sprinkle with sea salt. Scatter the garlic, spices, herbs and chilli (if using) over the pumpkin flesh.

Tear off two large sheets of foil and form them into two rings just smaller than the pumpkin halves. Place the foil rings on a large baking tray and position the pumpkin halves on top (this stops them sticking to the tray).

Roast for 20 minutes to get some colour, then reduce the oven temperature to 160°C (fan-forced) and cook for a further 40 minutes or until the pumpkin is soft but not falling apart.

Finish by drizzling with the sherry vinegar and a good amount of extra-virgin olive oil.

LEFTOVERS

Turn any leftover pumpkin into a delicious pumpkin and miso soup. Simply place the pumpkin, skin and all, in a saucepan and cover with chicken stock. Stir through 2 heaped tablespoons of miso paste and bring to the boil. Squeeze in the juice of 1 lemon, then remove from the heat, roughly blitz and serve with crusty bread.

MY FAVOURITE MASH, FROM AN IRISHMAN

SERVES 4–6

Mashed potato, done right. Enough said.

1 kg small–medium desiree
  potatoes, quartered
sea salt and freshly ground
  black pepper
80 g salted butter
250 ml (1 cup) full-cream
  milk, warmed
1½ tablespoons extra-virgin olive oil
3–4 tablespoons grated parmesan

Place the potato in a large saucepan and cover with cold water. Season with salt, then bring to the boil over medium–high heat. Reduce the heat to a simmer and cook until the potato is soft and a knife slips easily through the flesh.

Drain the potato and return it to the pan. Place the pan back on the warm stovetop to allow the potato to steam – this helps to dry out any excess moisture. As the potato steams, add the butter and let it melt.

Using a potato masher, mash the potato and butter and season with salt and pepper.

Swap the potato masher for a spatula and gradually add the warm milk, beating the mash as you go. If the mash seems too wet, simmer over low heat to remove any excess liquid until you are left with a creamy consistency.

Add the olive oil and cheese and check that you're happy with the seasoning.

Serve the mash with pretty much everything!

This mash is particularly delicious served with my fish pie (page 102) or meatloaf (page 168). Enjoy!

GREEN GNOCCHI

SERVES 6–8

This dish is a great way to sneak some extra greens onto your kids' plates. I've kept it simple here and served the gnocchi with olive oil, lemon zest and juice and parmesan, but you can also pair it with a tomato sauce or loads of grated cheese.

350 g rock salt
1.2 kg desiree potatoes,
    scrubbed clean
bunch of sage, leaves picked
bunch of flat-leaf parsley,
    leaves picked
½ bunch of rosemary, leaves picked
110 g (¾ cup) plain flour, plus extra
    for dusting
200 g parmesan, grated, plus extra
    to serve
sea salt and freshly ground
    black pepper
3 egg yolks
juice of 1 lemon
extra-virgin olive oil, for drizzling

Preheat the oven to 180°C (fan-forced).

Spread the rock salt out on a baking tray in an even layer. Place the potatoes on top, then dry in the oven for 1 hour to remove their moisture.

Cut the potatoes in half while they are still hot and push them through a potato ricer into a large bowl.

Place the herbs, flour, parmesan and a pinch of salt in a blender and blitz until well combined and bright green.

Add the egg yolks to the potato and use a spatula to chop through until they are just combined (this helps to hold the gnocchi together when boiling). Add the herb mixture and use the same chopping motion to combine the ingredients into a loose dough.

Flour your hands and a clean work surface to prevent the dough from sticking, then tip out the dough and use your hands to gently knead and bring it together without overworking it (this will result in tough gnocchi). You should have a soft, bright green dough.

Break off a portion of dough and gently roll it into a 1.5 cm-thick sausage. Cut the sausage into 2 cm-long pillows of gnocchi and set aside on a lightly floured tray. Repeat with the remaining dough.

Bring a large saucepan of salted water to the boil over medium–high heat. Reduce the heat to a simmer, then gently add the gnocchi to the pan. Watch and wait for them to rise to the top, then give them 30 seconds floating at the surface. Remove the gnocchi with a slotted spoon, allowing any excess water to drain away, and transfer to a serving bowl.

Drizzle the gnocchi with the lemon juice and olive oil, scatter over the lemon zest and extra parmesan, season with salt and freshly ground black pepper and serve.

OUR PERFECT PIZZAS

MAKES 10 SMALL–MEDIUM PIZZAS

I was given a portable pizza oven for Christmas and decided it was a great way to show the kids what actually goes into making a pizza. This dough recipe makes fantastic pizza bases, as well as flatbreads for dips or to serve with antipasti.

In this recipe, I've included a roasted tomato sauce, along with my favourite pizza toppings. There's also a recipe for hummus and a garlic and cumin oil, which you can brush onto the cooked dough to make a flavoursome flatbread. Meanwhile, the kids can argue over whether pineapple should be on or off the pizza.

330 ml warm water
35 g instant dried yeast
2 tablespoons caster sugar
1 kg baker's flour, plus extra
    for dusting and kneading
1 tablespoon sea salt
1 tablespoon olive oil
chopped rosemary leaves, to serve
rock salt, for sprinkling

ROASTED TOMATO SAUCE
3 ripe oxheart tomatoes
8 garlic cloves, unpeeled
8 baby (pearl) onions, unpeeled
½ bunch of thyme
½ bunch of rosemary
extra-virgin olive oil, for drizzling
10 basil leaves, roughly chopped
sea salt and freshly ground
    black pepper
splash of white wine vinegar

SMOKY HUMMUS FOR DIPPING
800 g canned chickpeas,
    drained and rinsed
4 garlic cloves, crushed
100 g tahini
1 teaspoon smoked paprika
2 teaspoons ground cinnamon
juice of 1 lemon
130 ml extra-virgin olive oil
1 bird's eye chilli, roughly chopped
1 tablespoon Greek yoghurt
sea salt
sesame seeds, to serve

Place the warm water, yeast and sugar in a bowl and whisk to combine. Set aside in a warm place for 20–30 minutes, until the yeast activates and starts to bubble.

Combine the flour and salt in a large mixing bowl.

Add the olive oil to the yeast mixture, then slowly add the mixture to the flour, mixing with your hand as you go. When all the liquid is incorporated into the flour, tip the dough onto a clean work surface lightly dusted with flour.

With floured hands, knead the dough for 5 minutes or until it becomes smooth and elastic. Keep dusting the dough as you knead to stop it sticking. Form the dough into a large ball, then dust the large bowl, add the dough ball and cover with a damp cloth. Set aside in a warm place for 30–40 minutes, until doubled in size.

Meanwhile, make the roasted tomato sauce. Preheat the oven to 180°C (fan-forced).

Place the tomatoes, garlic and onions in a deep roasting tin, scatter over the thyme and rosemary and drizzle with olive oil. Cover the tin with foil, then transfer to the oven and roast for 30–35 minutes, until the tomatoes, garlic and onions are soft and starting to collapse.

Set aside until cool enough to handle, then peel the onions and squeeze the garlic cloves from their skins. Place the onion, garlic and tomatoes in a large bowl and use a fork to gently break up the tomato and onion and combine. Add the basil, season with salt and pepper, then splash in a little white wine vinegar, to taste.

If you'd like to make the smoky hummus, place all the ingredients except the sesame seeds in the bowl of a food processor and blend until smooth. Taste and adjust the seasoning if necessary. Transfer to a bowl and scatter the sesame seeds over the top.

GARLIC AND CUMIN OIL
200 ml olive oil
2 tablespoons cumin seeds
4 garlic cloves, finely sliced

TOMATO AND MORTADELLA (MAKES 1 PIZZA)
3 tablespoons roasted tomato sauce
2 slices of mortadella, roughly torn
½ ball buffalo mozzarella, roughly torn

MARGHERITA (MAKES 1 PIZZA)
3 tablespoons roasted tomato sauce
½ ball buffalo mozzarella, roughly torn
basil leaves, to serve

If you'd like to make the garlic and cumin oil, place the olive oil, cumin and garlic in a small saucepan and heat until 60°C on a kitchen thermometer. Set aside.

Preheat the oven to as 250°C (fan-forced) or as high as it will go. Place a pizza stone or a pizza tray in the oven to heat up. Alternatively, you can use an electric pizza oven if you have one handy.

Re-knead the dough back to its original size, then divide the dough into 10 equal-sized pieces and roll them into balls. Working with one dough ball at a time and keeping the rest of the dough covered, roll the dough ball into a circle the same size as a dinner plate. If you're going to use the pizza base as a flatbread for serving with the hummus or brushing with the garlic and cumin oil, then very carefully transfer the base to the hot pizza stone or tray and cook for 4–5 minutes, until the pizza base is crisp. Cut the pizza base into slices and serve with the hummus for dipping, or brush the pizza base with the garlic and cumin oil, scatter the rosemary and salt over the top, then slice and serve.

Alternatively, add the toppings of your choice, then very carefully transfer to the hot pizza stone or tray and cook for 4–5 minutes, until the pizza base is crisp and the cheese is starting to melt.

Cut the pizza into slices and serve to the first lucky recipients. Continue to make pizzas using up the remaining dough and your chosen ingredients.

Any leftover hummus will keep in an airtight container in the fridge for up to 1 week. Leftover garlic and cumin oil will keep in an airtight container the fridge for up to 3 months, so long as the solids remain covered by the oil.

Lily & Maeve's Tip

The margherita is Maeve's fave.

SEAFOOD

TURMERIC CREAM MUSSELS

SERVES 4

Fresh turmeric is increasingly easy to find at supermarkets, and in this dish it adds an incredible depth of flavour to the mussels, bringing together the earth and the sea with a generous helping of cream. Serve with crusty bread to soak up the delicious sauce.

3 tablespoons coconut oil
1 onion, sliced
8 garlic cloves, chopped
1 tablespoon grated fresh turmeric
¼ bunch of thyme
200 ml white wine
1 litre pouring cream
2 kg mussels, cleaned and debearded
 (discard any that don't open when
 tapped on a work surface),
1 lemon, halved
crusty bread, to serve

Heat the oil in a frying pan over low heat. Add the onion, garlic, turmeric and thyme and cook, stirring occasionally, for 4–5 minutes, making sure the ingredients don't colour.

Pour in the wine and stir to deglaze the pan. Cook until the wine has reduced by two-thirds, then add the cream, bring to the boil and cook until the cream has reduced by one-quarter. Strain the liquid into a large stockpot.

Add the mussels to the pot, pop the lid on and bring to the boil. Cook for 2 minutes, then churn up the mussels with a wooden spoon and remove and reserve any that have opened. Continue to cook, stirring occasionally, for another 2 minutes until all the mussels have opened.

Remove the pot from the heat and discard any mussels that haven't opened. Divide the opened mussels and sauce among serving bowls, squeeze over the lemon halves and serve with crusty bread.

TIP

Keep the soaking water the mussels came in. I like to strain it, then add it to the sauce for an extra taste of the sea.

ISAAC'S CLAM PASTA

SERVES 8

This is a quick midweek meal that keeps the whole family happy. Clams are probably my favourite shellfish, I absolutely love them. When they are in season, I like to buy Cloudy Bay diamond shell clams from my mate Isaac in New Zealand. They are readily available from fishmongers, as well as being meaty and full of flavour. I love to use sorrel in this dish as it adds a punch of acidity to every bite.

1 kg clams
80 ml (⅓ cup) extra-virgin olive oil, plus extra for drizzling
1 red onion, finely diced
1 fennel bulb, finely diced
3 garlic cloves, finely sliced
20 g ginger, finely sliced
1 teaspoon chilli flakes
1 teaspoon fennel seeds
150 ml white wine
20 g butter
500 g dried spaghetti
juice of 1 lemon
bunch of sorrel, leaves picked
½ bunch of tarragon, leaves picked
½ bunch of flat-leaf parsley, leaves picked
sea salt and freshly ground black pepper (if needed)

Place the clams in a large bowl and cover with cold water. Set aside for 1 hour to purge them of any sand and grit. Drain and set aside.

Heat the olive oil in a large frying pan over low heat. Add the onion, fennel, garlic and ginger and cook, stirring occasionally, for 5 minutes or until the onion and fennel are soft.

Add the chilli flakes and fennel seeds and stir until the aroma of the fennel seeds fills the kitchen, then pour in the wine and stir to deglaze the pan. Add the butter, then tip in the drained clams and give the pan a good shake. Cover with a lid and cook for 4–5 minutes, until the clams open (discard any that don't).

Meanwhile, bring a large saucepan of water to the boil. Season generously with salt, then add the pasta and cook according to the packet instructions.

Squeeze the lemon juice over the opened clams and stir through the sorrel, tarragon and parsley leaves. Drizzle over a little olive oil and mix well to combine. Check the seasoning and adjust if necessary.

Drain the pasta and toss it through the clam mixture. Divide the pasta and clams among shallow bowls and serve immediately.

PRAWN BISQUE

SERVES 10

I call this Boxing Day soup as it's a great way to use up all the prawn heads and shells left over from Christmas Day. Serve it for lunch with crusty bread, then keep any leftovers to stir through pasta for a super-simple midweek supper.

300 g raw prawn heads and shells
   (save the prawns for another meal)
2 onions, roughly chopped
2 carrots, roughly chopped
1 celery stalk, roughly chopped
200 ml white wine
3 star anise
4 lemongrass stalks, white part only,
   roughly chopped
200 g ginger, roughly chopped
6 makrut lime leaves, roughly chopped
250 g canned diced tomatoes
300 ml pouring cream
zest and juice of 1 lemon
200 ml good-quality orange juice
   (freshly squeezed if possible)
sea salt and freshly ground
   black pepper

Place the prawn heads and shells in a very large heavy-based saucepan over medium heat. Cook, stirring, for 5 minutes or until the heads and shells turn orange and start to crisp, then add the onion, carrot and celery and cook for 10 minutes or until softened.

Add the white wine, star anise, lemongrass, ginger and lime leaves and bring to the boil, then add the tomatoes, cream and 2 litres of water. Bring the mixture back to the boil, then reduce the heat to low and simmer for 35–40 minutes, occasionally skimming off any scum that forms on the surface.

Strain the bisque into a clean saucepan and discard the solids (keep some lime leaves to serve, if you like). Set the pan over low heat, stir through the lemon zest and juice and orange juice and warm through.

Season to taste with salt and pepper, then divide among bowls, finish with a grinding of black pepper and serve.

> ## TIP
> The prawn bisque will keep in an airtight container in the fridge for up to 3 days or in the freezer for up to 1 month.

SUPER-CRISPY TEMPURA-STYLE FISH WITH TARTARE SAUCE

SERVES 6

Some batters can end up gluggy and soggy, completely ruining your fish and chips, but coating the fish in a tempura-style batter results in crisp, lightly fried fish every time. Served with homemade tartare sauce, this dish hands-down beats any takeaway version.

2 litres vegetable oil
100 g cornflour
100 g (⅔ cup) plain flour, plus extra
    for dusting
100 g tapioca flour
1 teaspoon bicarbonate of soda
sea salt and freshly ground
    black pepper
500 ml (2 cups) chilled soda water
6 flathead fillets, cut into thick strips
lemon halves, to serve

TARTARE SAUCE
250 g (1 cup) whole-egg mayonnaise
50 g salted baby capers, rinsed and
    drained, finely chopped
50 g cornichons, rinsed and drained,
    finely chopped
bunch of flat-leaf parsley, leaves
    roughly chopped, stalks finely
    chopped
zest and juice of 1 lemon
pinch of cayenne pepper

To make the tartare sauce, combine all the ingredients in a small bowl. Set aside in the fridge to chill until needed.

Meanwhile, preheat the oil in a deep-fryer or large heavy-based saucepan to 170°C on a kitchen thermometer.

Combine the cornflour, plain flour, tapioca flour and bicarbonate of soda in a large bowl. Season with salt and pepper and pour in the chilled soda water. Whisk the mixture to remove any lumps – the batter should have the consistency of milk.

Place enough flour to dust the fish strips on a large plate, then dredge the fish in the flour. Working with one fish strip at a time, dip the fish into the batter until completely coated. Carefully lower the fish into the hot oil and hold it for 3–4 seconds to allow it to sizzle before letting go (this helps the fish float and not stick to the bottom of the fryer or pan).

Fry the fish strips, using a slotted spoon to move them around now and again, for 4–5 minutes or until the batter is crisp and the fish is cooked through.

Remove the fish from the oil with the slotted spoon and drain on a plate lined with paper towel.

Divide the fish among plates, season with salt and pepper and serve with the tartare sauce and lemon halves on the side.

BAKED BABY SNAPPER WITH CHORIZO, CHERRY TOMATOES AND CAPSICUM

SERVES 2–3

This whole fish stew is my ode to the Mediterranean: fresh, light and thoroughly delicious. Fish on the bone always tastes better.

80 ml (⅓ cup) extra-virgin olive oil
1 mild chorizo sausage, diced
1 onion, roughly diced
3 garlic cloves, roughly chopped
160 g baby red capsicums,
    halved lengthways
300 g cherry tomatoes
120 ml white wine
½ bunch of tarragon, leaves picked
½ bunch of basil, leaves picked,
    plus extra to serve
1 x 600 g whole baby snapper,
    cleaned
lemon halves, to serve

Preheat the oven to 220°C (fan-forced).

Heat the olive oil in a large frying pan over low heat. Add the chorizo and cook, stirring occasionally, until lightly caramelised. Add the onion, garlic and capsicum and cook for 4–5 minutes or until soft, then add the cherry tomatoes and toss through to combine.

Pour in the white wine and stir to deglaze the pan, then bring the mixture to the boil and add 120 ml of water. Bring the mixture back to the boil, then reduce the heat to a simmer and cook for 10 minutes.

Throw in the herbs and continue to cook, stirring occasionally, for 2–3 minutes, until the tomatoes have collapsed and the mixture becomes stew-like. Spoon half the tomato mixture onto the base of a small roasting tin and place the snapper on top. Cover the fish with the remaining tomato sauce, then transfer to the oven and cook for 10 minutes or until the snapper has a core temperature of 50°C on a kitchen thermometer.

Remove the tin from the oven and allow to rest for 5 minutes, then scatter with extra basil, take to the table and serve with lemon halves on the side.

JOHN DORY WITH SEAWEED BUTTER

SERVES 4

I love to serve fish whole. Not only does it look impressive, it helps the fish retain its moisture during cooking. The seaweed butter is super easy to prepare and adds a delicate earthiness to this dish. This is truly a king of fish.

1 x 800 g whole John Dory, cleaned

SEAWEED BUTTER
10 g freshly grated horseradish root
10 g dried wakame
20 g ginger, grated
juice of 2 lemons
200 g salted butter, softened
3 teaspoons white wine vinegar
1 teaspoon caster sugar
pinch of sea salt

Preheat the oven to 200°C (fan-forced).

To make the seaweed butter, blitz all the ingredients in the small bowl of a food processor.

Spread a little of the seaweed butter over the base of a small roasting tin that will snugly fit the fish. Place the John Dory on top, then liberally spread the rest of the seaweed butter over the fish.

Bake in the oven for 20–25 minutes, until the fish reaches a core temperature of 50°C on a kitchen thermometer.

Rest the fish for 8 minutes before serving.

MISO-GLAZED MACKEREL

SERVES 4

I have used blue mackerel fillets in this dish, but this fantastic miso glaze works equally well with other fish fillets, vegetables or meat.

4 x 100 g blue mackerel fillets,
   skin on, pin-boned
lime wedges, to serve
A Simple Green Salad (see page 21),
   to serve

MISO GLAZE
50 g white miso paste
50 g salted butter, softened
1 bird's eye chilli, roughly chopped
juice of 1 lime
2 garlic cloves, roughly chopped
20 g ginger, roughly chopped
1 teaspoon fish sauce
1 teaspoon sesame oil

Preheat the oven grill to high.

To make the miso glaze, place all the ingredients in the small bowl of a food processor, add a splash of water to help loosen the ingredients and blitz to a paste.

Place the mackerel fillets, skin-side down, on a baking tray and liberally brush the miso glaze over the top. Transfer to the grill and cook for 3–4 minutes, until the fish is cooked through and the miso glaze is caramelised.

Divide the mackerel among plates and serve with lime wedges and my simple green salad.

WHOLE STEAMED FLOUNDER WITH FENNEL

SERVES 2

If you're nervous about cooking whole fish, I recommend starting with flounder, as it's very simple to prepare and the cooked flesh comes away easily from the bone. I like to steam flounder in the oven with fennel and Pernod, which imparts a delicate aniseed flavour. Give it a go!

1 large potato, peeled and cut into
   3 cm-thick slices
200 ml white wine
90 ml Pernod
sea salt and freshly ground
   black pepper
stalks and fronds from 4 fennel bulbs
   (see Leftovers below)
1 x 800 g whole flounder (or 2 smaller
   flounder), cleaned
1 lemon, finely sliced
2 teaspoons fennel seeds
3 fresh bay leaves
6 lemon thyme sprigs
6 garlic cloves, finely sliced

Preheat the oven to 180°C (fan-forced).

Arrange the potato slices over the base of a roasting tin large enough to fit the flounder (the potato acts as a base to prevent the fish from overcooking).

Combine the wine and Pernod with 1 litre of water in a saucepan. Season with salt and bring to the boil, then pour the mixture into the roasting tin and scatter half the fennel stalks and fronds over the potato and liquid.

Lay the flounder on the fennel and season with salt and pepper. Top with the lemon slices, fennel seeds, bay leaves, lemon thyme, garlic and the remaining fennel tops. Cover the tin tightly with foil and bake for 30 minutes or until the thickest part of the flesh behind the head reaches 48–50°C on a kitchen thermometer.

Remove the tin from the oven and allow the flounder to rest, uncovered, for 5 minutes. Transfer the fish to a serving dish and strain the juices from the tin into a small jug.

Serve the flounder with the pan juices drizzled over the top.

LEFTOVERS

Use some of the leftover fennel bulbs to make a simple fennel and pea salad. Shave one large or two small fennel bulbs into a salad bowl and toss through a handful of fresh peas. Drizzle over some of the vierge dressing on page 21 and toss to coat. Serve with the flounder.

CITRUS FISH SOUP

SERVES 8

When I ran the Four in Hand in Sydney, we served this soup as a complimentary amuse-bouche at the start of every meal. I tried to change the menu once, but it didn't go down well, so we brought it back and it stayed there until the day we closed. I always choose sustainable fish whenever possible and leatherjackets are a great option with healthy ocean stocks. They're also cheap to buy and readily available at good fishmongers. If you can't get hold of them, this soup works just as well with firm white fish fillets.

80 ml (⅓ cup) extra-virgin olive oil
1 large onion, roughly chopped
2 fennel bulbs, roughly chopped
2 garlic bulbs, unpeeled, halved
    horizontally
100 g ginger, roughly chopped
50 g fennel seeds
3 star anise
4 whole leatherjackets or
    similar-sized sustainable
    fish, cleaned
200 ml white wine
800 g canned diced tomatoes
1 litre good-quality orange juice
    (freshly squeezed if possible)
250 ml (1 cup) pouring cream,
    plus extra to serve
4 bay leaves (fresh if possible)
bunch of thyme
sea salt and freshly ground
    black pepper
crusty bread, to serve

Heat the olive oil in a very large saucepan or stockpot over low heat. Add the onion, fennel, garlic, ginger, fennel seeds and star anise and cook, stirring occasionally, for 2–3 minutes, until the onion and fennel are soft.

Add the fish and cook for 3–4 minutes, then pour in the wine and stir to deglaze the pan. Add the tomatoes, orange juice, cream, bay leaves, thyme and 4 litres of water. Bring the mixture to the boil, then reduce the heat to a simmer and cook for 1 hour or until the liquid has reduced by one-third.

Stir the soup with a spoon to break up the fish, then strain through a coarse colander into a large jug. Discard the solids. Season to taste with salt and pepper, then divide the soup among bowls (check that no bones have slipped through the colander) and serve with an extra drizzle of cream, a grinding of pepper and crusty bread on the side.

You can also use the soup as a delicate poaching liquid to cook other fish of your choice.

DECADENT FISH PIE

SERVES 6

This fish pie is a fantastic way to incorporate a variety of seafood in one dish. Feel free to swap out the prawns, scallops and fish depending on what is available at your local fishmonger. Serve with my mashed potato for a hearty and comforting meal.

100 ml olive oil
1 onion, finely diced
1 fennel bulb, finely diced
3 garlic cloves, finely chopped
200 ml Pernod
65 g salted butter, roughly chopped
65 g plain flour
300 ml fish stock
300 ml full-cream milk
200 g raw prawns, peeled
   and deveined
150 g scallops, halved, roe removed
150 g firm white fish fillet, skin off,
   pin-boned, roughly chopped
150 g flaked smoked fish
½ bunch of dill, fronds picked and
   finely chopped
½ bunch of chives, finely snipped
2 sheets good-quality frozen puff
   pastry, just thawed
1 egg, beaten with a splash of
   full-cream milk
handful of thyme leaves (optional)
My Favourite Mash (see page 71),
   to serve
lemon halves, to serve

Heat the olive oil in a large frying pan over medium heat. Add the onion, fennel and garlic and cook, stirring occasionally, for 5–8 minutes, until the onion and fennel are soft but not coloured. Pour in the Pernod and stir to deglaze the pan. Add the butter and flour and cook, stirring, for 5 minutes.

Meanwhile, pour the fish stock and milk into a saucepan and bring to the boil. Add the prawns, scallops, white fish and smoked fish, reduce the heat to a simmer and poach for 2 minutes. Remove from the heat and set aside.

Ladle half the poaching liquid into the pan with the vegetables and stir over medium heat for 10 minutes, until reduced and thick.

Gently remove the seafood from the poaching liquid and add it to the pan with the vegetables, being careful not to stir too vigorously to avoid breaking up the fish. Stir through the dill and chives.

Preheat the oven to 220°C (fan-forced).

Check the consistency of the remaining poaching liquid – it should coat the back of a spoon – and if it's too runny, place it back over medium heat and cook until further reduced.

Transfer the fish pie filling to a 35 cm x 25 cm (or similar) baking dish and pour over the reduced poaching liquid. Cut the puff pastry sheets so they are just larger than the dimensions of your pie dish, then carefully lay them slightly overlapping over the pie filling and crimp the edges to seal. Poke a small hole in the centre for steam to escape and brush with the egg wash. Sprinkle with the thyme leaves, if using.

Allow the egg wash to dry for 10 minutes (this will give you a glossy finish), then transfer the dish to the oven and bake for 15 minutes. Reduce the temperature to 180°C (fan-forced) and cook for a further 15 minutes or until the pastry is puffed and golden.

Allow the pie to rest for 10 minutes, then divide among plates and serve with my favourite mash and lemon halves for squeezing.

This chapter features the most-cooked dish in our house (page 110) and my daughters' hands-down favourite meal (page 112).

CHICKEN
& DUCK

CFC - COLIN'S FRIED CHICKEN

SERVES 6-8

The secret to juicy fried chicken is to soak the fillets first. I like to use buttermilk, which adds acidity and provides a wonderful foil against the spicy, crisp crumb. Some might almost say they are finger lickin' good! Get the kids involved in the flouring process, but turf them out of the kitchen when it's time to deep-fry.

6–8 chicken thigh fillets, skin on
260 ml buttermilk
2 litres vegetable or sunflower oil
sea salt and freshly ground
    black pepper
Smoky Mayo (see page 60), to serve
green salad leaves, to serve
FRIED CHICKEN SPICE MIX
300 g (2 cups) plain flour
100 g cornflour
1 tablespoon smoked paprika
2 teaspoons onion powder
2 teaspoons garlic powder
2 teaspoons cayenne pepper
1 tablespoon ground cumin
2 teaspoons ground turmeric
2 teaspoons ground coriander
1 teaspoon dried Italian herbs

Place the chicken in a large bowl and cover with the buttermilk. Cover and set aside in the fridge to marinate for at least 6 hours or overnight.

Heat the oil in a deep-fryer or large saucepan to 180°C on a kitchen thermometer.

Combine all the chicken spice mix ingredients in a small bowl, then spread the mixture out on a clean tray.

Remove the chicken from the fridge and drain away the excess buttermilk. Roll each chicken thigh through the spice mix until well-coated, then leave to sit in the spice mix for 30 minutes to absorb the flavours.

Working in batches, gently lower the chicken into the hot oil and cook, turning occasionally, for 5 minutes or until golden and crisp and the internal temperature is 60°C on a kitchen thermometer.

Using a slotted spoon, remove the chicken from the hot oil and drain on a wire rack with paper towels underneath to soak up the excess oil.

Transfer the fried chicken to a serving bowl and serve with my smoky mayonnaise on the side for dipping and green salad leaves for freshness.

GREEN CHICKEN CURRY

SERVES 4

This is my version of Thai green chicken curry that's light-tasting while still being big on flavour. The amount of chillies in this dish will result in a medium-heat curry, so feel free to add more or less depending on how hot you like things.

1 tablespoon coconut oil
500 ml (2 cups) coconut milk
1 cinnamon stick
2 star anise
250 ml (1 cup) good-quality
   chicken stock
6 makrut lime leaves
splash of white wine vinegar
4 chicken thighs, bone in, skin on
1 lime, halved
steamed jasmine rice, to serve

GREEN CURRY PASTE
2 bunches of coriander, roots
   scraped clean, stalks and leaves
   roughly chopped (reserve a few
   leaves to serve)
6 long green chillies, sliced
   lengthways and deseeded
2 red bird's eye chillies,
   sliced lengthways
4 red onions, roughly chopped
6 garlic cloves, roughly chopped
6 makrut lime leaves, roughly chopped
2 bunches of Thai basil, leaves picked
   and roughly chopped (reserve a
   few leaves to serve)
2 lemongrass stalks, white part only,
   roughly chopped
100 g ginger, roughly chopped
100 g galangal, roughly chopped
1 tablespoon coriander seeds,
   toasted
1 teaspoon caster sugar
3 tablespoons fish sauce

To make the green curry paste, place all the ingredients in a blender or the small bowl of a food processer and blitz to a smooth paste, adding a splash of water to get things going if necessary.

Heat the coconut oil in a large frying pan over medium heat. Add half of the green curry paste (freeze the rest to use another time) and cook, stirring, for 2 minutes or until aromatic. Add the coconut milk, cinnamon and star anise and simmer for 10 minutes, then add the stock, lime leaves and white wine vinegar and simmer for a further 10 minutes.

Add the chicken to the pan and simmer for 20 minutes or until the chicken is cooked through. Squeeze the lime halves over the top, then divide the chicken and curry among bowls, top with extra coriander and Thai basil leaves, and serve with steamed jasmine rice on the side.

SOY-POACHED CHICKEN

SERVES 4-6

This is the most-cooked dish in our house! It's my go-to meal when I want something that's light, but still packed full of flavour. The end result is melt-in-the-mouth chicken that's perfect served with steamed rice. Turn any leftover chicken into a salad the next day with home-made salad cream using the tip below. This recipe also works well with pork fillet. Add the pork as soon as the liquid comes to the boil, then remove from the heat (no need to simmer).

130 g ginger, roughly chopped
bunch of coriander, roots scraped clean, leaves picked
1 tablespoon sesame oil
2 tablespoons chilli oil, such as chiu chow
80 g coconut oil
2 lemongrass stalks, white part only, smashed using the side of a knife
2 onions, roughly chopped
2 carrots, roughly chopped
2 garlic bulbs, halved horizontally
2 bay leaves (fresh if possible)
4 makrut lime leaves
1 cinnamon stick
4 star anise
200 ml white wine
200 ml light soy sauce
2½ tablespoons fish sauce
2½ tablespoons Chinese black vinegar
50 g dried shiitake mushrooms
3 tablespoons brown sugar
1 x 1.6 kg free-range chicken
4–6 eggs
steamed white rice, to serve
crispy fried shallots, to serve

Place the ginger, coriander root, sesame oil, chilli oil and half the coconut oil in the small bowl of a food processor and blitz to a rough paste.

Heat the remaining coconut oil in a large saucepan over medium heat. Add the paste and lemongrass, and cook, stirring, for 2 minutes or until fragrant. Add the onion, carrot, garlic, bay leaves, lime leaves, cinnamon and star anise and cook, stirring frequently, for 4 minutes or until the onion and carrot are soft but not turning brown.

Pour in the wine and stir to deglaze the pan, then add the soy sauce, fish sauce, Chinese black vinegar and dried shiitake mushrooms, along with 2 litres of water. Bring to the boil and add the sugar, then reduce the heat and simmer for 20 minutes. Add the chicken to the pan, making sure it is submerged under the liquid, and bring everything back to the boil. Reduce the heat to very low, add one egg for each guest and simmer for 9 minutes.

Remove the pan from the heat, then cover and allow the chicken to poach in the liquid for 1–1½ hours, until the chicken is firm and the juices run clear when the thickest part of the thigh is pierced with a knife.

To serve, remove the chicken from the liquid and cut into portions. Peel the eggs and slice them in half.

Divide steamed white rice among serving bowls and top with the chicken, egg, a handful of crispy shallots and a few coriander leaves. Spoon over a little of the poaching liquid and serve immediately.

LEFTOVERS

Turn leftover chicken into a salad for lunch the next day. Make a simple salad cream by combining 250 g mayo, 25 ml evaporated milk and 2 teaspoons white wine vinegar. Season with caster sugar and salt and set aside. Shred the leftover chicken into a bowl and add a handful of chopped tarragon, basil and rocket leaves, along with 3 tablespoons chopped capers. Squeeze over ½ lemon, season and lightly coat in salad cream. Serve on large lettuce leaves.

BAD BOYS (AKA CRISPY CHICKEN THIGHS)

SERVES 4

This adaptation of my famous chicken bread recipe has quickly become a family favourite at home, and was given its name by my daughters, Lily and Maeve. It's easier to prepare than the original, requires less cooking time and the portion sizes are more manageable, but that doesn't stop my kids fighting over how much crispy skin they get!

4 chicken thighs, bone in, skin on
80 g salted butter, softened
1 garlic bulb, cloves peeled and
    smashed using the side of
    a large knife
1 loaf good-quality sourdough
1 potato, sliced
bunch of basil
bunch of thyme
bunch of tarragon
300 ml extra-virgin olive oil
sea salt and freshly ground
    black pepper
1 lemon, halved

CHICKEN BRINE
50 g table salt
1 tablespoon brown sugar

To brine the chicken, pour 1 litre of water into a large container and stir through the salt and sugar until dissolved. Add the chicken thighs and set aside in the fridge for 3 hours.

Preheat the oven to 200°C (fan-forced).

Pat the chicken thighs dry with paper towel and discard the brine. Combine half the butter and half the garlic in a small bowl, then slide the mixture over the chicken skin. Using your hands, smooth the skin to spread the butter mixture around the thighs.

Cut the sourdough loaf in half horizontally and set the top half aside for another use. Arrange the potato slices in the base of a roasting tin and sit the bread on top. Rip the herbs, then scatter them over the bread (set aside a few thyme sprigs for later), along with the remaining garlic cloves. Cut the remaining butter into small pieces and dot over the top. Drizzle with half the olive oil and season with salt and pepper.

Place the chicken thighs on top of the bread, drizzle over the remaining oil, top with the remaining thyme sprigs and season again.

Roast for 40 minutes or until the chicken is cooked through and golden. Remove the tin from the oven and rest the chicken for 10 minutes. Squeeze over the lemon halves.

Divide the potato, chicken and bread among plates and serve.

Lily & Maeve's Tip

This is the best dish our dad cooks!

CHICKEN TERRINE

SERVES 6-8

This chicken terrine is an elegant way to start a dinner, or serve it as a light lunch with a crisp, green salad. It's soft, rich and packed full of flavour. This recipe needs to be started the day before.

8 chicken marylands

1.5 litres vegetable oil, extra-virgin olive oil or duck fat (I like to use half duck fat, half extra-virgin olive oil)

bunch of tarragon, leaves picked and roughly chopped

bunch of sage, leaves picked and roughly chopped

bunch of flat-leaf parsley, leaves picked and roughly chopped

3 tablespoons baby capers, rinsed and drained, chopped

100 ml sherry vinegar

sea salt and freshly ground black pepper

Celery Salad with Vierge Dressing (see page 16), to serve

toasted or grilled bread, to serve

Preheat the oven to 90°C (fan-forced). Line a terrine mould or dish with enough plastic wrap to overhang all the way around. If you are going to serve the terrine straight from the mould, don't line it with plastic – the terrine can be scooped out with a spoon.

Place the chicken marylands in a large flameproof casserole dish. Add the oil or fat to the pan, then cover with foil and place in the oven for 3 hours to gently cook.

To check that the chicken is cooked, carefully remove a leg using a slotted spoon and place it on a chopping board. Gently push the meat with a knife – it should easily fall off the bone. If it doesn't, place the dish back in the oven for a further 30 minutes or until the meat falls easily off the bone.

Remove the dish from the oven and allow the confit chicken to cool to room temperature in the fat. Remove the chicken from the fat, then pick the meat from the bones, being careful not to mush it up too much. Discard the fat and bones.

Combine the chicken, herbs, capers and sherry vinegar in a large bowl. Taste, then season with salt and pepper.

Start to pack the chicken mixture into the lined terrine mould or dish, pressing down firmly to remove any air bubbles. Continue to fill the mould until all the mixture is used up, then fold the overhanging plastic wrap over the mixture and place a tray with a weight on top to help compress the terrine. Set aside in the fridge to chill overnight.

The next day, turn out the terrine onto a plate (or scoop straight from the mould or dish), then slice and serve with the celery salad and lots of toasted or grilled bread.

CHICKEN SCHNITZEL AND SLAW

SERVES 4

The humble chicken schnitzel is a firm pub favourite, but when it comes to recreating it at home it's surprising how many of us struggle to achieve the same result. So here is my foolproof chicken schnitty recipe that's packed with texture and flavour. I highly recommend serving it with my zingy cabbage and fennel slaw – it makes the perfect accompaniment.

4 chicken breast fillets
300 g (2 cups) plain flour
sea salt and freshly ground
    black pepper
3 eggs
splash of full-cream milk
1.5 litres vegetable or canola oil
Cabbage and Fennel Slaw
    (see page 27), to serve
lemon wedges, to serve

SCHNITZEL CRUMB
500 g dried breadcrumbs
½ bunch of sage, leaves picked
    and finely chopped
100 g (½ cup) red quinoa
200 g (2 cups) rolled oats
100 g poppy seeds
sea salt and freshly ground
    black pepper

To make the schnitzel crumb, combine all the ingredients in a large bowl and set aside.

Slice through each chicken breast horizontally, being careful not to slice all the way through, then open up the fillets so they look like a book. Working with one chicken breast at a time, place each fillet between two large sheets of plastic wrap and gently bash with a small mallet or rolling pin until 5 mm to 1 cm thick. Be careful not to bash the fillets too thinly, otherwise they will fall apart when cooking.

Place the flour in a large bowl and season well with salt and pepper. Whisk together the beaten egg and milk in a separate large bowl.

Heat the oil in a deep-fryer or large saucepan to 180°C on a kitchen thermometer.

Working with one schnitzel at a time, dredge the chicken in the seasoned flour, then coat in the egg wash. Transfer to the bowl with the schnitzel crumb and press the mixture onto the chicken until completely coated. For an extra-crispy schnitzel, return the chicken to the egg wash, then coat in another layer of the schnitzel crumb.

Add the schnitzels, one by one, to the hot oil and cook, turning occasionally, for about 5 minutes, until crisp and golden on the outside with an internal temperature of 60°C on a kitchen thermometer.

Using a slotted spoon, remove the schnitzels from the oil and drain on paper towel. Keep warm.

Season the schnitzels with salt and pepper, then transfer to plates and serve with the slaw and lemon wedges on the side for squeezing over.

TIP!

Any leftover schnitzel crumb can be frozen for next time.

SALT-CRUSTED CHICKEN

SERVES 4

This is a chicken in an oven, in an oven! The salt crust dough encases and lightly steams the chicken, while imparting a gentle herb and salt flavour. Crack this open at the table for a super-impressive reveal.

1 x 1.6 kg free-range chicken
olive oil, for brushing
freshly ground black pepper
3 garlic cloves, finely chopped
2 teaspoons salted butter, softened

SALT CRUST
1 kg plain flour, plus extra for dusting
300 g table salt
½ bunch of rosemary, leaves picked
   and roughly chopped
½ bunch of marjoram, leaves picked
   and roughly chopped
½ bunch of thyme, leaves picked
3 egg whites

To make the salt crust, combine the flour, salt and chopped herbs in a large bowl.

Beat the egg whites in another bowl and stir through 300 ml of cold water until well combined. Pour the liquid into the middle of the flour mixture and bring everything together to form a rough dough. Transfer the dough to a floured work surface and knead for 5 minutes or until soft. Cover with plastic wrap and set aside in the fridge for 1 hour.

Place the chilled dough on a floured work surface and roll out to a 2 cm-thick circle, large enough to wrap the chicken.

Brush the chicken with olive oil and season with pepper, then rub the garlic and butter all over the chicken.

Preheat the oven to 180°C (fan-forced). Line a baking dish with baking paper.

Place the chicken in the centre of the salt crust dough, then gently lift and mould the crust around the chicken and seal at the top. Patch up any holes with leftover bits of dough.

Carefully transfer the chicken parcel to the prepared dish and bake for 1 hour or until the thickest part of the chicken thigh reaches 60°C on a kitchen thermometer (you will need to pierce the salt crust to do this).

Allow the chicken to rest for 15–20 minutes, then crack open the salt crust, carve the chicken into thick slices and serve.

This salt crust can also be used to cook whole baby barramundi. Simply clean and descale your baby barra, then cover the fish with the salt crust and bake for 40 minutes.

DUCK CONFIT WITH LENTILS DU PUY

SERVES 4

This is an elegant, yet robust, classic French dish that's rich in flavour. You will need to start this recipe one day ahead, but it's well worth the effort for the sophisticated end result. The lentils du puy is a great side that also pairs well with any number of meat dishes in this book.

4 duck legs
1.5 litres vegetable oil, extra-virgin olive oil or duck fat (I like to use half duck fat, half extra-virgin olive oil)
splash of extra-virgin olive oil

DUCK SALT RUB
zest of 3 oranges
3 star anise
2 cinnamon sticks
4 garlic cloves, finely sliced
100 g coarse salt
30 g brown sugar
pinch of freshly grated nutmeg
10 g black peppercorns, crushed
3 bay leaves (fresh if possible)
pinch of fennel seeds

LENTILS DU PUY
500 g puy lentils
80 ml (⅓ cup) extra-virgin olive oil
1 onion, finely diced
2 carrots, finely diced
1 garlic bulb, unpeeled, halved horizontally
3 bay leaves (fresh if possible)
½ bunch of thyme
200 ml red wine
1 litre good-quality chicken or ham-hock stock
30 g salted butter
1½ tablespoons sherry vinegar (or apple cider vinegar)
sea salt and freshly ground black pepper

To make the duck salt rub, blitz all the ingredients in a spice grinder until coarsely blended. Massage the rub into the duck legs, then set aside in the fridge, uncovered, for 4 hours.

Preheat the oven to 90°C (fan-forced).

Brush the rub off the duck legs, then place the legs in a flameproof casserole dish. Add the oil or fat to the dish, then cover with foil and place in the oven for 3 hours to gently cook.

To check that the duck legs are cooked, carefully remove a leg using a slotted spoon and place it on a chopping board. Gently push the meat with a knife – it should easily fall off the bone. If it doesn't, place the dish back in the oven for a further 30 minutes or until the meat falls easily off the bone.

Remove the dish from the oven and allow the confit duck to cool to room temperature in the fat. Remove the duck from the fat, then place, skin-side down, on a tray and place another tray on top. Weigh the top tray down with something heavy, such as a few cans of beans, then set aside in the fridge overnight. This helps to give the duck a flat surface, which will result in a wonderfully crispy skin when you cook it a second time.

The next day, preheat the oven to 160°C (fan-forced).

To make the lentils du puy, place the lentils in a heavy-based saucepan and pour in enough cold water to just cover. Place over high heat and bring to the boil (this removes any impurities that could taint the finished dish). Drain the lentils and set aside.

Wipe out the pan, then pour in the olive oil and set over medium heat. Add the onion, carrot, garlic and herbs and cook for 5 minutes or until the vegetables are just starting to soften. Pour in the red wine and stir to deglaze the pan, then bring to the boil. Add the blanched lentils and stock, then bring to a gentle simmer and cook for 30–35 minutes until the lentils are al dente.

Meanwhile, heat a small splash of olive oil – you only need a little as a lot of fat will be released from the duck – in an ovenproof frying pan over high heat. Place the duck, skin-side down, in the pan, then transfer to the oven and cook for 20–25 minutes, until the skin is golden and crisp and the meat is completely soft.

Stir the butter through the lentils until melted, then splash in the sherry vinegar, season with salt and pepper and give everything a good stir.

Divide the duck and lentils among plates and serve.

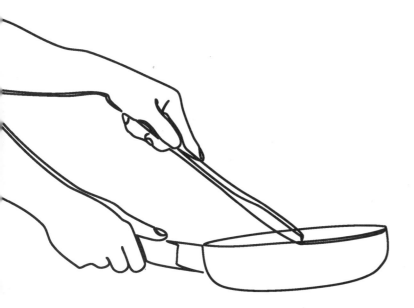

PORK

MY PORK AND FENNEL SAUSAGE ROLLS

SERVES 2-4

There isn't much that beats light, crispy pastry wrapped around full-flavoured pork mince. These sausage rolls are a poor man's dish elevated to new heights. I love to serve them with gentleman's relish, an old-fashioned paste made with anchovies, but good old tomato relish works just as well. Double the recipe to make extra like we have here – they freeze well.

1 tablespoon extra-virgin olive oil
2 onions, finely chopped
½ bunch of sage, leaves picked and
   roughly chopped
4 garlic cloves, roughly chopped
2 tablespoons fennel seeds, crushed,
   plus extra to sprinkle
1 teaspoon smoked paprika
1 teaspoon cayenne pepper
1 teaspoon freshly grated nutmeg
1 teaspoon ground ginger
200 g pork mince
100 g minced pork back fat
100 g fresh breadcrumbs
1 egg yolk
sea salt and freshly ground
   black pepper
1 sheet good-quality frozen puff
   pastry, just thawed
gentleman's relish (see Tip) or your
   favourite relish, to serve
1 egg, lightly beaten

Heat the olive oil in a large frying pan over medium heat. Add the onion, sage, garlic and fennel seeds and cook, stirring occasionally, for 5 minutes or until the onion is soft. Stir through the smoked paprika, cayenne pepper, nutmeg and ginger, then remove from the heat, transfer to a large bowl and set aside to cool.

Add the pork mince, pork back fat and breadcrumbs to the cooled onion mixture and use your hands to bring everything together. Add the egg yolk, season well with salt and pepper and mix again until completely combined.

Transfer the mixture to a clean tray and roll it into a 12 cm-long log, about 2 cm wide. Loosely cover with paper towel, then set aside in the fridge for at least 30 minutes to firm up.

Preheat the oven to 180°C (fan-forced). Line a baking tray with baking paper.

Cut the puff pastry to the same length as your rolled sausage meat, then carefully place the chilled sausage meat along the length of pastry closest to you. Gently lift the pastry over the sausage meat and carefully roll it up into one large sausage roll. Brush all over with the beaten egg and sprinkle with salt and pepper and extra fennel seeds.

Transfer the sausage roll to the prepared baking tray and bake for about 15 minutes, until the pastry is golden and the sausage meat reaches 60°C on a kitchen thermometer.

Allow the sausage roll to cool slightly, then cut into your desired lengths. Serve with relish.

Also known as patum peperium, gentleman's relish is a strong-tasting paste made from anchovy fillets, butter, herbs and spices. It is available from some delicatessens and online.

HERB-CRUMBED PORK CUTLETS

SERVES 4

Some might call these posh schnitties. Crumbing pork cutlets is a great way to add texture and flavour to an otherwise simple dish. Scattering a little grated apple over the pork before serving adds a wonderful fresh crunch that cuts through the richness of the pork.

plain flour, for dusting
2 eggs
400 ml full-cream milk
4 x 200 g pork cutlets, bone in,
    fat removed
100 ml olive oil
grated granny smith apple, to serve
ZEST AND HERB CRUMB
150 g (1½ cups) dried breadcrumbs
zest of 1 lemon
¼ bunch of rosemary, leaves picked
    and finely chopped
¼ bunch of sage, leaves picked and
    finely chopped
¼ bunch of marjoram, leaves picked
    and finely chopped
50 g (½ cup) grated parmesan
1 tablespoon mustard seeds
1 tablespoon fennel seeds, crushed
    using a mortar and pestle
freshly ground black pepper

Preheat the oven to 200°C (fan-forced).

To make the zest and herb crumb, combine all the ingredients in a large shallow bowl. Place enough flour to dust the cutlets in a separate shallow bowl and whisk together the eggs and milk in a third bowl.

Dust the cutlets in the flour to coat, then dip in the egg wash. Transfer to the zest and herb crumb and firmly press the crumbs into the cutlets until completely coated. Set aside.

Heat the olive oil in a large ovenproof frying pan over medium heat. Add the cutlets and cook for 2 minutes on each side, until just starting to brown. Transfer to a wire rack, place in the oven and cook for 6–8 minutes, or until the cutlets are crisp and golden on the outside and pink in the middle with an internal temperature of 58°C on a kitchen thermometer. Remove from the oven and transfer the cutlets to paper towel to drain.

Cut the zested lemon in half and squeeze the juice over the cutlets. Scatter a little grated apple over the top and serve.

CHORIZO AND WHITE BEAN BAKE

SERVES 6

This bean bake is a one-pot wonder, and the end results are like a moreish warm hug. You can serve it on its own or as an accompaniment to your choice of protein. Alternatively, leave to cool, then toss through a dressing and serve as a salad or follow the tip below to transform it into a hearty soup. This is another dish that tastes even better the next day. You will need to start this recipe the day before you want to eat it.

300 g dried white cannellini beans, soaked in cold water overnight
80 ml (⅓ cup) extra-virgin olive oil
4 spicy chorizo sausages, roughly chopped
100 g smoked pancetta, fat removed, roughly chopped
3 red onions, roughly chopped
1 garlic bulb, unpeeled, halved horizontally
4 red capsicums, roughly diced
2 carrots, roughly chopped
1 fennel bulb, roughly chopped
2 bay leaves (fresh if possible)
bunch of thyme, leaves picked
1 teaspoon smoked paprika
1 teaspoon cayenne pepper
1 teaspoon fennel seeds
100 ml white wine
400 ml passata

CHEESY BREADCRUMB AND SAGE TOPPING
100 g fresh breadcrumbs
100 g (1 cup) grated parmesan
bunch of sage, leaves picked

Drain the beans and give them a good rinse, then tip them into a large heavy-based saucepan and cover with cold water. Bring to a simmer over medium heat and cook, uncovered, for about 1 hour or until the beans are soft but not mushy. Remove from the heat and set aside. Do not drain.

Preheat the oven to 180°C (fan-forced).

Heat the olive oil in a flameproof casserole dish over low heat. Add the chorizo and pancetta and cook for 3–4 minutes, then increase the heat to high and cook for a further 2–3 minutes to give them a good bit of colour.

Reduce the heat to medium, then add the onion, garlic, capsicum, carrot, fennel and herbs. Cook, stirring, for 5 minutes or until soft, then stir through the smoked paprika, cayenne and fennel seeds. Pour in the wine and stir to deglaze the dish, then add the passata, the beans and just enough of their cooking water to moisten the mixture. Stir well to combine.

To make the cheesy breadcrumb and sage topping, place all the ingredients in a blender and blitz until you have a fine green crumb. Tip the mixture onto the beans and spread out in an even layer.

Transfer the casserole dish to the oven and bake for 40 minutes or until the topping is crisp and golden.

Before serving, fish out the garlic halves and squeeze over the soft roasted garlic.

LEFTOVERS

If you have leftovers, this bake makes a fantastic hearty soup for lunch the next day. Place the leftover bake in a saucepan and cover with good-quality chicken stock. Bring the mixture to the boil, then remove from the heat and blitz using a hand-held blender into a smooth soup. Serve with crusty bread.

SCOTCH EGGS

SERVES 6

Scotch eggs are classic pub fare and in this recipe I've given them an Asian twist. Serve with pickles and your favourite beer.

9 eggs
splash of full-cream milk
500 g pork mince
50 g minced pork back fat
20 g ginger, finely chopped
   or grated
2 garlic cloves, finely chopped
   or grated
2 teaspoons sesame oil
1½ tablespoons soy sauce
vegetable oil, for deep-frying
200 g (1⅓ cups) plain flour
300 g fresh breadcrumbs
pickles of your choice, to serve

Bring a saucepan of water to the boil and add six of the eggs. Cook for 6 minutes, then drain and allow to cool slightly. Very carefully peel the eggs (they will be delicate as they are soft-boiled) and set aside.

Whisk the remaining eggs and milk in a small bowl and set aside.

Combine the pork, pork fat, ginger, garlic, sesame oil and soy sauce in a large bowl, then divide the mixture into six portions. Again working very carefully, mould the mince mixture around each egg until completely coated in an even layer.

Heat enough oil for deep-frying in a deep-fryer or large saucepan to 160°C on a kitchen thermometer.

Place the flour and breadcrumbs in separate shallow bowls. Roll the coated eggs in the flour, then dip in the egg wash and roll in the breadcrumbs until completely coated. Repeat this process to double-crumb the eggs.

Working in batches, deep-fry the Scotch eggs for 5 minutes, turning frequently, until golden and cooked through. Drain the Scotch eggs on a plate lined with paper towel.

Serve warm with pickles.

MILK-POACHED PORK NECK WITH SOFT CHEESY POLENTA

SERVES 4–6

This is a an old-fashioned way to cook pork. The milk softens and mellows the flavour of the pork, while the pork enriches the milk. Don't be alarmed if the milk splits and forms a cheese-like curd during cooking. This is completely normal and the flavour will not be compromised. Served with soft and cheesy polenta, this soothing dish is comfort food at its best.

100 ml olive oil
1 x 600 g pork neck
1 onion, chopped
1 garlic bulb, unpeeled, halved
   horizontally
½ bunch of thyme
½ bunch of rosemary
½ bunch of sage, plus extra
   leaves, torn, to serve
2 bay leaves (fresh if possible)
300 ml white wine
about 1.5 litres full-cream milk
1 parmesan rind (optional)
sea salt and freshly ground
   black pepper

SOFT CHEESY POLENTA
800 ml good-quality chicken stock
   or water
250 ml (1 cup) full-cream milk
1 parmesan rind (see Tip)
150 g (1 cup) polenta
½ bunch of thyme, leaves picked
1 bay leaf (fresh if possible)
60 g grated parmesan, plus extra
   to serve
120 g salted butter, chopped
zest and juice of 1 lemon
sea salt and freshly ground
   black pepper

Preheat the oven to 140°C (fan-forced).

Heat the olive oil in a flameproof casserole dish over medium heat. Add the pork neck and sear on all sides for 8–10 minutes, until golden brown. Add the onion, garlic and herbs and cook, stirring, for 5 minutes or until soft. Pour in the wine and stir to deglaze the pan, then add the milk and parmesan rind (if using) and season with salt and pepper. The pork neck should be submerged in the milk, so add a little more if needed.

Cover the dish, then place in the oven and cook for 3 hours or until the pork neck is soft enough to break up with a spoon. Remove from the oven and rest the pork in the milk for 40 minutes.

Meanwhile, to make the cheesy polenta, place the chicken stock or water, milk and parmesan rind in a saucepan and bring to the boil over medium heat.

Whisk in the polenta and add the thyme and bay leaf. Reduce the heat to low and simmer, whisking constantly, for 30–40 minutes, until the polenta is thick and creamy.

Whisk in the grated parmesan, butter and lemon zest and squeeze in the lemon juice. Discard the parmesan rind and bay leaf. Check the seasoning and adjust if necessary.

Squeeze the roasted garlic into the poaching liquid and stir through. Carve the pork neck into thick slices and divide among plates, along with the polenta. Scatter extra grated parmesan and sage leaves over the polenta and spoon some of the poaching liquid over the pork.

TIP

If you don't have a parmesan rind to hand for the polenta, simply throw an extra handful of grated parmesan into the milk.

CLASSIC MEATBALLS

SERVES 6

This is a great dish to get the kids involved, as they can get their hands messy mixing and rolling the meatballs. It's a versatile and forgiving recipe, so don't stress if you're missing the odd herb. Simply swap it out for one that you have or use extra of any of the below. Easy!

300 g veal mince
300 g pork mince
½ bunch of tarragon, leaves picked
   and roughly chopped
½ bunch of basil, leaves picked and
   roughly chopped
½ bunch of flat-leaf parsley, leaves
   picked and roughly chopped
½ bunch of marjoram, leaves picked
   and roughly chopped
30 g fresh breadcrumbs, softened
   in a splash of milk
1 egg
sea salt and freshly ground
   black pepper
125 ml (½ cup) extra-virgin olive oil
1 onion, finely chopped
4 garlic cloves, finely sliced
1 x quantity Roasted Tomato Sauce
   (see page 77)
800 g canned diced tomatoes
grated parmesan, to serve

Place the veal and pork mince in a large mixing bowl and, using your hands, mix through the herbs. Add the softened breadcrumbs and egg and mix until completely combined. Season with salt and pepper, mix again, then cover and set aside in the fridge for 1 hour for the flavours to come together.

Heat 2 tablespoons of the olive oil in a frying pan over medium heat. Add the onion and garlic and cook, stirring occasionally, for 5 minutes or until the onion is soft and translucent. Remove from the heat and set aside to cool.

Add the cooled onion mixture to the rested mince, then, using your hands, massage and work the mince mixture until completely combined. Using wet hands, roll the mixture into golf ball–sized balls, then place on a tray and set aside in the fridge for 1 hour to firm up.

Preheat the oven to 180°C (fan-forced).

Heat the remaining olive oil in a large heavy-based frying pan over high heat. Working in batches, add the meatballs and cook, rolling them around in the pan to colour, for 2–3 minutes or until browned all over.

Transfer the seared meatballs to a baking dish, pour over the roasted tomato sauce and canned tomatoes and bake, uncovered, for 30–40 minutes, until the meatballs are cooked through and the sauce is bubbling.

Rest the meatballs in the dish for 10 minutes, then sprinkle over the cheese and serve.

WHOLE PORK BELLY ROASTED OVER VEG

SERVES 8-10

A family favourite through and through. I like to gently roast the pork belly on top of the vegetables, as it imparts a sweetness, along with the pork's fantastic flavour. Like the chorizo and white bean bake on page 133, any leftovers can be transformed into a salad or soup the next day. This recipe needs to be started two days ahead.

1 x 1.6 kg good-quality
   boneless pork belly
sea salt and freshly ground
   black pepper
6 carrots, unpeeled
12 baby (pearl) onions, unpeeled
2 fennel bulbs, halved lengthways
4 small garlic bulbs, unpeeled
splash of extra-virgin olive oil
4 bay leaves (fresh if possible)
½ bunch of sage
½ bunch of thyme
½ bunch of marjoram
pinch of freshly grated nutmeg
pinch of ground cinnamon
pinch of fennel seeds
150 ml sweet cider

Score the pork skin at 1 cm intervals, then rub a liberal amount of salt into the skin. Place the pork, skin-side up, on a tray and place in the fridge, uncovered, for 2 days.

Preheat the oven to 260°C (fan-forced) or as high as your oven will go.

Toss the vegetables with a good splash of olive oil in a large roasting tin, then scatter over the herbs (reserving a few sprigs of thyme) and spices and lay the pork belly, skin-side up, on top. Scatter over the remaining thyme and grind over some pepper.

Transfer the tin to the oven and roast for 40 minutes, then lower the heat to 180°C (fan-forced) and cook for a further 1 hour or until the pork is cooked through and the crackling is super crisp. Remove the pork from the tin and set aside to rest. Return the tin to the oven and cook the veg for a further 10–15 minutes, until golden.

Squeeze the roasted garlic bulbs over the veg, pour in the cider and toss to combine. Thickly slice the pork belly and serve with the vegetables and juices from the pan drizzled over the top.

LEFTOVERS

Use leftovers to make a simple and hearty salad by chopping up the leftover pork belly and vegetables and tossing them in my green sauce that goes with everything (see page 34). Transfer to a salad bowl and serve straight away. Alternatively, follow the leftovers instructions on page 133 to make a delicious soup.

ONE-PAN BAKED CHORIZO, HALOUMI AND TOMATO

SERVES 4

This is my go-to entree when people come over for dinner. Serve it in the middle of the table in the pan and let everyone help themselves. Don't forget the flatbread to mop up the juices at the end – they're the best bit! This also works as a weekend lunch for two.

2 tablespoons extra-virgin olive oil
100 g mild chorizo sausages,
   thickly sliced
180 g buffalo haloumi, or similar
   good-quality haloumi
1 garlic clove, finely chopped
1 bird's eye chilli, finely chopped
16 cherry tomatoes
1 rosemary sprig, leaves picked
6 sage leaves
1 marjoram sprig, leaves picked
juice of 1 lemon
flatbreads, to serve

Preheat the oven to 180°C (fan-forced).

Heat the olive oil in an ovenproof frying pan over medium heat. Add the chorizo and sauté for 3–4 minutes, until caramelised, then add the haloumi and cook until the underside is just golden. Turn the haloumi over and add the garlic, chilli and tomatoes, then transfer the pan to the oven and cook for 5 minutes or until the haloumi is oozing and soft.

Remove the pan from the oven and toss through the rosemary, sage and marjoram, allowing the leaves to blister in the hot oil.

Squeeze over the lemon juice, then take the pan to the table and invite everyone to help themselves. Serve with plenty of your favourite flatbreads.

STICKY PORK RIBS IN BARBECUE SAUCE

SERVES 4–6

I first created this recipe at 4Fourteen using lamb ribs, but I switched to pork ribs for family dinners as they were easier to get hold of. Whichever ribs you choose to use, it's the shiny, sticky glaze that will keep you coming back for more. It's out-of-this-world good.

2 litres sugar-free cola
500 ml (2 cups) barbecue sauce
500 ml (2 cups) tomato passata
100 ml sriracha chilli sauce
400 ml apple cider vinegar
3 tablespoons onion powder
3 tablespoons garlic powder
3 tablespoons smoked paprika
2 cinnamon sticks
5 star anise
3 teaspoons fish sauce
sea salt and freshly ground
    black pepper
3 kg pork rib racks

Preheat the oven to 120°C (fan-forced).

Combine all the ingredients except the salt and pepper and pork ribs in a very large flameproof casserole dish set over medium heat. Bring to the boil and cook for 20 minutes or until the liquid has reduced by half. Season to taste with salt and pepper.

Cut the pork rib racks in half to help them fit in the dish, then submerge the ribs in the sauce.

Cut a piece of baking paper the same size as the inside of your dish and carefully lay it over the ribs (this is called a cartouche). Seal the dish with a layer of foil, then pop the lid on to tightly seal. Transfer to the oven and cook for 1¼ hours, then remove the lid, foil and baking paper and continue to cook the ribs for another 1¼ hours or until the meat is falling off the bone. Remove, and allow the pork ribs to cool in the cooking liquid, uncovered, for 1 hour.

Meanwhile, ladle one-third of the cooking liquid into a saucepan and cook over medium heat for 20 minutes or until the sauce has reduced by half to a thick and glossy glaze.

Preheat the oven to 200°C (fan-forced).

Place the ribs in a large roasting tin, making sure they are not overlapping. Spoon over half the reduced glaze, then transfer to the oven and cook for 10 minutes or until the ribs are lovely and sticky. Remove the ribs from the oven and spoon the remaining glaze over the top, then cook for a further 10 minutes.

Serve immediately.

This sticky glaze is great for a Christmas ham.

PORCHETTA

SERVES 10

This porchetta is such a crowd pleaser at dinner parties, and you'll hear many 'oohs' and 'aahs' as you carve through the pork. Succulent meat, fragrant stuffing, crispy skin. Heaven. Serve with a simple green salad to let the porchetta shine. You will need to start this recipe the day before.

1 x 2.5 kg pork belly
80 ml (⅓ cup) extra-virgin olive oil, plus extra for rubbing
80 g salted butter
1 large onion, finely sliced
1 garlic bulb, cloves peeled and roughly chopped
2 green apples, grated
1 tablespoon fennel seeds
250 g fresh breadcrumbs
bunch of sage, leaves picked and roughly chopped
½ bunch of rosemary, leaves picked and roughly chopped
½ bunch of flat-leaf parsley, leaves picked and roughly chopped
½ bunch of silverbeet, stalks and leaves roughly chopped
500 g pork sausage mince
1 teaspoon ground ginger
1 teaspoon freshly grated nutmeg
1 teaspoon ground cinnamon
1 teaspoon smoked paprika
1 teaspoon cayenne pepper
sea salt
green salad leaves, to serve

Place the pork belly, skin-side up, in the fridge uncovered and leave overnight to air-dry.

The next day, heat the olive oil and butter in a large frying pan over medium heat. Add the onion, garlic, apple and fennel seeds and cook, stirring occasionally, for 5 minutes or until the onion is soft and translucent. Remove the pan from the heat and stir through the breadcrumbs, then set aside to cool.

Preheat the oven to 250°C (fan-forced) or as high as your oven can go.

Place the cooled onion and breadcrumb mixture in a food processor, along with the herbs and silverbeet, and blitz until well combined. Transfer the mixture to a large bowl and, using your hands, mix through the sausage mince, spices and a good pinch of salt until completely combined.

Remove the pork belly from the fridge and lay on a clean work surface, skin-side down, with a long edge facing you. Spread the sausage and herb mixture over the pork belly in an even layer, making sure it is no higher than 5 mm.

Starting with the edge closest to you, roll the pork belly as tightly as possible into a large sausage, then tie the roll using kitchen string at 2 cm intervals, trying to keep the roll as tight as possible as you go.

Lightly rub the rolled pork with olive oil, then transfer to a wire rack set over a roasting tin and roast for 25 minutes or until the skin starts to crackle and blister. Reduce the temperature to 170°C (fan-forced) and roast for a further 45 minutes or until the porchetta's core temperature is 60°C on a kitchen thermometer.

Allow the porchetta to rest for 30 minutes, then cut into thick slices and serve with a green salad.

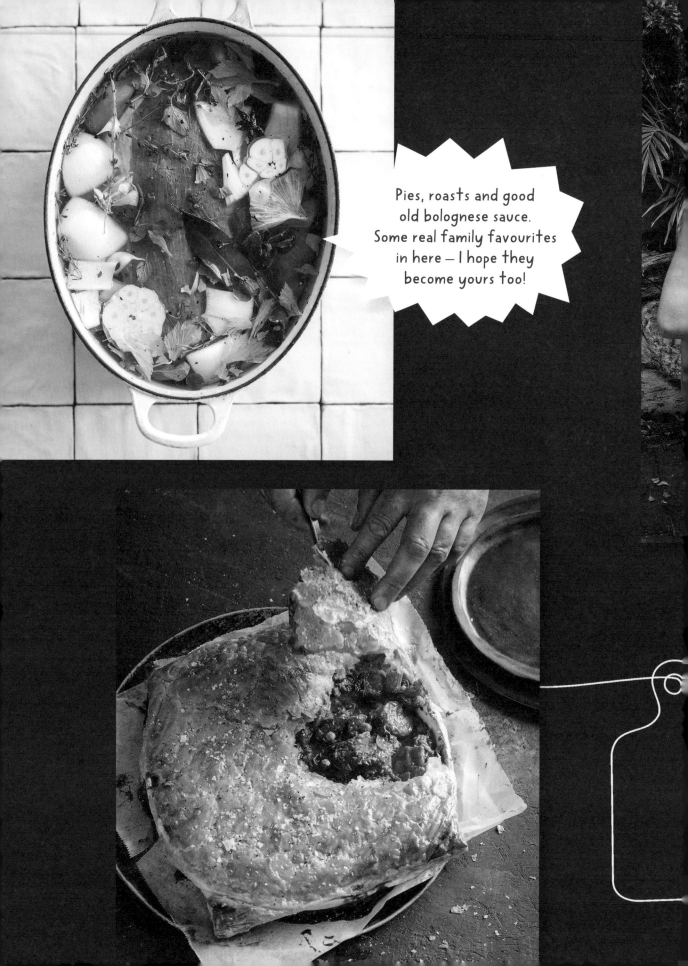

Pies, roasts and good
old bolognese sauce.
Some real family favourites
in here – I hope they
become yours too!

RED MEAT

SHEPHERD'S PIE WITH CRUSHED KIPFLER CRUST

SERVES 6

This hearty staple is a firm family favourite. I've given this shepherd's pie the Fassnidge treatment by using the mighty kipfler potato instead of regular mash. Give it a go!

2½ tablespoons olive oil
500 g lamb mince
sea salt and freshly ground
   black pepper
3 carrots, finely diced
1 fennel bulb, finely diced
bunch of spring onions,
   finely chopped
2 celery stalks, finely diced
4 garlic cloves, finely sliced
1 tablespoon fennel seeds
½ bunch of marjoram, leaves
   picked and chopped
2 fresh bay leaves, torn
60 g plain flour
2½ tablespoons red wine vinegar
200 ml red wine
400 g can diced tomatoes
2 tablespoons dijon mustard
500 ml (2 cups) good-quality
   chicken stock

CRUSHED KIPFLER CRUST
8–10 kipfler potatoes
   (or use desiree potatoes)
sea salt and freshly ground
   black pepper
200 ml olive oil
1 teaspoon freshly grated nutmeg
1 egg, beaten
zest and juice of 1 lemon
50 g (½ cup) grated parmesan

Heat the olive oil in a large heavy-based frying pan over medium heat. Add the mince and spread it out in a single layer. Allow the mince to sear, without stirring, for 10–15 minutes to get some colour and caramelisation going, then stir and cook for 10 minutes, until the mince is browned all over. Season with salt and pepper, then add the vegetables and fennel seeds and cook, stirring, for 5 minutes. Add the marjoram and bay leaves and stir to combine, then sprinkle over the flour and stir to mix through.

Add the red wine vinegar and red wine and stir to deglaze the pan. Bring to the boil, then add the tomatoes and mustard and stir again. Pour in the chicken stock and cook, stirring occasionally, for 30 minutes, until the mixture thickens.

Transfer the mixture to a large baking dish, then set aside to cool.

Preheat the oven to 180°C (fan-forced).

To make the crushed kipfler crust, place the potatoes in a large saucepan and cover with cold water. Season with salt, then bring to the boil over medium–high heat. Reduce the heat to a simmer and cook the potatoes for 20–25 minutes, until they are soft and a knife slips easily through the flesh.

Drain the potatoes, then return them to the pan and place over low heat, allowing them to steam dry for 1–2 minutes. Using a fork, roughly crush the potatoes, then season with salt and pepper. Add the remaining crust ingredients and mix well to combine.

Liberally spread the crushed potato mixture over the lamb mince mixture, then transfer to the oven and cook for 40 minutes or until the crust is lightly golden.

Allow the shepherd's pie to rest for 10 minutes, then divide among plates and serve.

MY BOLOGNESE

SERVES AN ARMY

This is my go-to classic bolognese recipe, which the whole family loves, but here's a secret: it actually tastes better the next day. Served on top of pasta or a jacket potato with plenty of grated cheese, it really is one of life's simple pleasures.

This recipe calls for parmesan rind, a culinary trick employed by nonne all over Italy, who save this precious end of the cheese to add flavour and depth to sauces and soups. Keep your leftover cheese rinds in the freezer and pop one into any dish that could benefit from an umami boost.

100 ml extra-virgin olive oil
150 g pork mince
150 g beef mince
150 g chicken breast mince
2 onions, roughly chopped
2 celery stalks, roughly chopped
2 carrots, roughly chopped
100 g button mushrooms, sliced
1 garlic bulb, unpeeled, halved
  horizontally
200 ml white wine
1.5 litres passata
3 bay leaves (fresh if possible)
½ bunch of thyme, leaves picked
  and chopped
½ bunch of marjoram, leaves picked
  and chopped
parmesan rind
sea salt and freshly ground
  black pepper
good-quality cooked pasta of your
  choice, to serve
grated parmesan, to serve

Heat half the olive oil in a large heavy-based frying pan over medium–high heat. Add the pork, beef and chicken mince and cook, breaking up the mince with the back of a wooden spoon, for 15 minutes or until browned.

Meanwhile, in a separate large heavy-based frying pan, heat the remaining olive oil over low heat. Add the onion, celery, carrot, mushroom and garlic and cook, stirring occasionally, for 10 minutes or until the vegetables are soft.

Add the wine to the browned mince and stir to deglaze the pan, then tip the mince into the pan with the vegetables and stir well to combine. Pour in the passata and add the bay leaves, thyme, marjoram and parmesan rind. Season with salt and pepper.

Bring the mixture to a gentle simmer, then reduce the heat to the lowest setting possible and simmer for 1½ hours, stirring occasionally, until the bolognese is reduced and thick.

Towards the end of cooking, remove the garlic bulb halves from the sauce and set aside to cool a little. Pop the garlic cloves from their skins and return the soft, oozy garlic to the pan, stirring through. Discard the parmesan rind.

Serve the bolognese over your favourite pasta topped with plenty of grated parmesan.

Make more than you need and freeze the rest.

CORNED BEEF WITH OLD-SCHOOL PARSLEY SAUCE

SERVES 8

This one's dedicated to Jeremy Strode.

1 x 1.5 kg corned beef silverside, rinsed
2 carrots, roughly chopped
2 celery stalks, roughly chopped
2 onions, roughly chopped
1 garlic bulb, unpeeled, halved horizontally
2 star anise
4 bay leaves (fresh if possible)
bunch of thyme
100 ml white wine vinegar
1 teaspoon black peppercorns

PARSLEY SAUCE
50 g butter
50 g (⅓ cup) plain flour
700 ml full-cream milk
juice of 2 lemons
2 bunches of flat-leaf parsley, leaves picked and finely chopped
sea salt and freshly ground black pepper

Place all the ingredients except the parsley sauce in a large stockpot and set over low heat. Cover with water so that the corned beef is completely submerged, then bring to a gentle simmer. Cook for 4 hours or until a knife inserted into the corned beef slides through easily. (Keep an eye on the water level and top it up if it drops below the surface of the corned beef. This stops the beef drying out.)

Remove the pot from the heat and allow the corned beef to come to room temperature in the poaching liquid.

Meanwhile, to make the parsley sauce, melt the butter in a saucepan over medium heat. Stir in the flour, then reduce the heat to low and cook for 3–4 minutes, until the mixture looks like wet sand. Pour in all the milk and whisk constantly to prevent any lumps forming until the sauce starts to thicken. Bring the sauce to a simmer and continue to whisk for 5 minutes or until you have a smooth sauce. Add the lemon juice and parsley and stir well to combine. Taste, season with salt and pepper and set aside.

Remove the corned beef from the pot and drizzle over some of the poaching liquid. Slice the corned beef and divide among plates. Spoon over a generous amount of parsley sauce and serve with your favourite veg.

IRISH STEW IN OZ

SERVES 4

This is my ode to Ireland. I've lightened it a little to match the Australian climate, but it's still good ol' Irish stew. A heart-warming and much-loved classic.

80 ml (⅓ cup) extra-virgin olive oil
4 carrots, roughly chopped
4 celery stalks, roughly chopped
2 onions, roughly chopped
2 garlic bulbs, unpeeled, halved
    horizontally
3 bay leaves (fresh if possible)
bunch of marjoram
bunch of thyme
1 x lamb shoulder (about 1.5 kg),
    bone in
300 ml white wine
sea salt and freshly ground
    black pepper
6–8 kipfler potatoes
bunch of baby turnips, trimmed
1 swede, diced

Find a flameproof casserole dish big enough to fit the whole lamb shoulder, then add the olive oil and set the dish over low heat. Add the carrot, celery, onion and garlic and cook, stirring occasionally, for 5 minutes or until the vegetables are soft. Add the bay leaves, marjoram and thyme and cook, stirring, for a further 2 minutes or until their fragrance fills the kitchen.

Add the lamb shoulder to the dish but don't let it colour – this is a white stew so you don't want the lamb to brown. Pour in the wine and stir to deglaze the dish. Bring the mixture to the boil, then season generously with salt and pepper and pour in enough cold water to cover the lamb. Bring to the boil again, then reduce the heat to a simmer and cook, covered, for 2½ hours or until the lamb is almost cooked but not quite coming away from the bone.

Add the kipfler potatoes, turnips and swede to the dish and cook for 10 minutes or until the potatoes are cooked through and the lamb is fall-apart tender.

Remove the dish from the heat and allow the stew to rest for 30 minutes before serving.

SPICED CALF'S LIVER FOR MY DAD

SERVES 4

Dad always used to cook dinner on a Wednesday night and calf's liver was his go-to dish. Liver is so underrated in my opinion – it's affordable and a great source of iron and protein. I like to serve this with lentils du puy or a simple green salad.

100 g (⅔ cup) plain flour
1 tablespoon garlic powder
1 tablespoon onion powder
1 tablespoon ground cumin
1 tablespoon smoked paprika
1 tablespoon ground turmeric
pinch of sea salt
1 teaspoon chilli flakes
2 tablespoons vegetable oil
600 g calf's liver, trimmed and
    cut into 1.5 cm-thick slices
1 tablespoon butter
½ bunch of sage, leaves picked
Lentils du Puy (see page 123) or
    green salad leaves, to serve

Place the flour, garlic and onion powders, cumin, paprika, turmeric, salt and chilli flakes in the small bowl of a food processor and briefly blitz to combine. Transfer the mixture to a shallow bowl.

Heat the oil in a large frying pan over high heat. Working in batches, coat the calf's liver slices in the seasoned flour. Shake off any excess flour, then add to the hot pan and cook for about 1 minute on each side until just cooked through. Please don't overcook the liver, otherwise it will be tough – it should still be pink on the inside. When the liver is just cooked, add the butter and sage leaves and briefly cook until the bottom of the liver is just starting to caramelise.

Divide the liver among plates and serve with lentils du puy or your favourite green salad.

STEAK AND KIDNEY PIE

SERVES 4

This is hands-down my all-time favourite pie. So much so that it's probably my death-row meal. Thankfully, I've got my kids onto it as well, which allows me to put it on high rotation at home. Success!

100 ml olive oil
500 g chuck steak, diced
200 g kidneys, trimmed and diced
300 ml red wine
1 large onion, diced
1 large carrot, diced
1 celery stalk, diced
3 garlic cloves, finely chopped
1 swede, diced
3 bay leaves (fresh if possible)
¼ bunch of thyme, leaves picked
100 g salted butter
100 g (⅔ cup) plain flour
2½ tablespoons worcestershire
    sauce
1 tablespoon Vegemite
1 tablespoon dijon mustard
300 ml good-quality beef stock
sea salt and freshly ground
    black pepper
1 sheet good-quality frozen puff
    pastry, just thawed
1 egg, lightly beaten
sesame seeds, for sprinkling

Heat two-thirds of the olive oil in a flameproof casserole dish over high heat. Add the steak and sear on all sides until well browned, then add the kidney and cook for 2 minutes. Pour in the red wine and stir to deglaze the dish, then remove the steak, kidney and cooking juices from the dish and set aside.

Heat the remaining olive oil in the dish over medium heat. Add the onion, carrot, celery and garlic and cook for 4–5 minutes, until softened. Add the swede, bay leaves and thyme and cook for 5 minutes.

Meanwhile, melt the butter in a saucepan over medium heat. Rain in the flour and cook, stirring, for 4 minutes or until the mixture resembles wet sand. This is your roux.

Stir the roux through the dish, then add the worcestershire sauce, Vegemite and mustard. Stir for 1 minute, then add the beef stock and simmer for 30 minutes or until the stock has thickened and the swede has cooked through. Season with salt and pepper.

Preheat the oven to 220°C (fan-forced).

Return the steak and kidney to the dish, along with the deglazed juices, and stir until well combined. Transfer the mixture to a pie dish.

Trim the puff pastry to just larger than your pie dish, then lay the pastry over the filling and poke a small hole in the centre for steam to escape. Brush the pastry with beaten egg and allow to dry for 10 minutes before baking (this will give you a glossy finish). Sprinkle with sesame seeds.

Transfer the dish to the oven and cook for 15 minutes, then reduce the temperature to 180°C (fan-forced) and cook for a further 15 minutes until the pie is golden and bubbling.

Allow to cool for a few minutes, then slice and serve.

Lily & Maeve's Tip

Kidneys taste and feel just like mushrooms.

OSSO BUCCO

SERVES 4

Osso bucco: a heart-warming family favourite that feels like a warm hug from your favourite Italian (or Irish) nonna.

3 tablespoons extra-virgin olive oil
4 (about 1.8 kg) osso bucco
1 fennel bulb, roughly chopped
2 carrots, roughly chopped
2 onions, peeled and left whole
1 garlic bulb, unpeeled, halved
   horizontally
300 ml red wine
400 g can diced tomatoes
good-quality chicken stock, to cover
½ bunch of thyme
3 bay leaves (fresh if possible)
pinch of fennel seeds
2 star anise
splash of soy sauce

Preheat the oven to 160°C (fan-forced).

Heat the olive oil in a large flameproof casserole dish over medium–high heat. Add the osso bucco and seal the meat on all sides for 5–8 minutes until golden brown.

Add the fennel, carrot, onion and garlic and sauté for 5 minutes or until the vegetables start to brown. Pour in the red wine and stir to deglaze the dish, then stir through the tomatoes and bring to the boil. Pour enough chicken stock into the dish to cover the osso bucco and throw in the herbs, fennel seeds and star anise. Bring the mixture to the boil again, then stir through a generous splash of soy sauce.

Cover the dish and cook in the oven for 2 hours or until the osso bucco can be easily pulled apart with a fork. Squeeze the roasted garlic cloves into the dish and stir through.

Divide the osso bucco and vegetable mixture among plates and serve.

MY FAVOURITE MEATLOAF

SERVES AN ARMY

Meatloaf is sometimes looked down upon, but I disagree. I think it's high time we brought this iconic dish back to the family dinner table. Nutritious and filling, I believe everyone should know how to make a good meatloaf. This is another dish that I think tastes even better the next day.

80 ml (⅓ cup) extra-virgin olive oil, plus extra for drizzling
2 onions, finely diced
2 carrots, finely diced
2 celery stalks, finely diced
6 garlic cloves, finely sliced
300 g beef mince
300 g pork or veal mince
½ bunch of rosemary, leaves picked and finely chopped
½ bunch of thyme, leaves picked and finely chopped
100 g fresh breadcrumbs, soaked in a splash of milk
100 g (1 cup) rolled oats
50 g (⅓ cup) unsalted cashew nuts, roughly chopped
50 g (⅓ cup) almonds, roughly chopped
50 g (⅓ cup) shelled pistachio nuts, roughly chopped
50 g (⅓ cup) pine nuts, toasted
1 tablespoon fennel seeds
1 tablespoon ground cumin
1 teaspoon freshly ground nutmeg
2 large eggs, beaten
sea salt and freshly ground black pepper
My Favourite Mash (see page 71), to serve

MY MUSHY PEAS
1 tablespoon vegetable oil
1 onion, diced
4 garlic cloves, finely sliced
2 streaky bacon rashers, finely chopped
1 bay leaf (fresh if possible)
200 g green split peas
100 ml white wine
1 tablespoon salted butter
2½ tablespoons white wine vinegar
sea salt and freshly ground black pepper

Preheat the oven to 180°C (fan-forced). Line a large loaf tin with baking paper.

Heat the olive oil in a large heavy-based saucepan over low heat. Add the onion, carrot, celery and garlic and cook, stirring frequently, for 5 minutes or until the vegetables are soft. Remove from the heat and set aside to cool.

Place the cooled veg in a large mixing bowl and add the remaining ingredients except the mash. Using your hands, massage the ingredients together until they are very well combined, then spoon the mixture into the prepared tin, pressing down as you go to get rid of any air pockets. Season the top of the meatloaf and drizzle over a little olive oil.

Place the tin in a larger tin or baking dish and fill with enough water to come halfway up the side of the meatloaf. Transfer to the oven and bake for 40 minutes, then remove from the oven and allow the meatloaf to rest for 30 minutes.

Meanwhile, for the mushy peas, heat the oil in a large saucepan over low heat and add the onion, garlic, bacon and bay leaf. Cook, stirring frequently, for 5 minutes, then stir through the green split peas.

Add the white wine and bring to the boil, then pour in enough water to just cover the peas and bring to a simmer. Cook for 35–40 minutes, until the peas are soft, topping the water up from time to time if the pan starts to dry out.

Give the split peas a good stir to help break them up and become a little mushy. Add the butter and vinegar and season with salt and pepper, then transfer to a serving dish and drizzle with extra-virgin olive oil.

Cut the meatloaf into thick slices and serve with mashed potato and mushy peas.

Store any leftover meatloaf in an airtight container in the fridge for up to 1 week or in the freezer for up to 3 months.

OX TONGUE

SERVES 4

Ox tongue is a great introduction to nose-to-tail cooking and I encourage everyone to give it a go. This is an old-school recipe from my early restaurant days, but it's still a firm favourite. The ox tongue does take two days to prepare, but I hope you will agree that it's worth the effort. The end result is a sensational dish that can be served as a cold cut or chargrilled in a hot pan and served with my green sauce.

1 ox tongue
2 tablespoons extra-virgin olive oil
2 onions, halved
2 celery stalks, roughly chopped
2 carrots, roughly chopped
2 garlic bulbs, unpeeled, halved
   horizontally
2 star anise
1 cinnamon stick
2 bay leaves (fresh if possible)
200 ml white wine
200 ml red wine vinegar
A Green Sauce to Go With Everything
   (see page 34), to serve

BRINE
300 g table salt
200 g caster sugar
400 ml red wine vinegar
2 bay leaves (fresh if possible)
1 tablespoon black peppercorns
½ bunch of thyme
4 star anise
4 garlic cloves, peeled
1 cinnamon stick

To make the brine, place all the ingredients and 300 ml of water in a saucepan and bring to a simmer over medium heat. Stir until the salt and sugar have dissolved, then remove from the heat and set aside to cool to room temperature.

Transfer the brine to a large non-reactive container and submerge the tongue in the liquid. Set aside in the fridge for 2 days.

Heat the olive oil in a large heavy-based saucepan over low heat. Add the onion, celery, carrot and garlic and cook, stirring occasionally, for 5 minutes or until soft. Stir in the star anise, cinnamon and bay leaves, then add the white wine and stir to deglaze the pan.

Pour in the red wine vinegar and bring the mixture to the boil, then add the brined tongue and cover with enough cold water to submerge the tongue. Discard the brine.

Bring the mixture to a simmer and cook for about 1 hour or until the meat is soft to touch, but not too mushy.

Remove the pan from the heat and leave the tongue to cool in the liquid until it reaches room temperature. Discard the solids. Place the tongue on a chopping board and carefully peel off the skin and discard.

Store the tongue in the liquid in an airtight container in the fridge until ready to serve. It will keep for up to 1 week.

To serve, thinly slice the tongue and serve as a cold cut or cut into thick slices and chargrill in a hot pan until heated through. Serve with my green sauce.

LAMB SHANKS WITH HERBED COUSCOUS

SERVES 6

Shanks are an affordable cut of lamb that are full of flavour, and in this dish you get the double bonus of lamb stock from the slow-cooked meat. I use this stock to flavour and season the herbed couscous, which cuts through the richness of the lamb. This makes a wonderful Sunday lunch.

100 ml extra-virgin olive oil
6 lamb shanks
sea salt and freshly ground
   black pepper
2 onions, roughly chopped
2 carrots, roughly chopped
2 celery stalks, roughly chopped
1 garlic bulb, unpeeled, halved
   horizontally
2 star anise
1 tablespoon fennel seeds
1 tablespoon cumin seeds
1 bay leaf (fresh if possible)
½ bunch of rosemary sprigs
½ bunch of thyme sprigs
200 ml white wine
800 g canned diced tomatoes
3 litres good-quality chicken stock
   or water

HERBED COUSCOUS
250 g couscous
2½ tablespoons extra-virgin olive oil
juice of 1 lemon
½ bunch of basil, leaves picked
   and roughly chopped, plus extra
   leaves to serve
½ bunch of tarragon, leaves picked
   and roughly chopped
sea salt and freshly ground
   black pepper

Preheat the oven to 180°C (fan-forced).

Heat the olive oil in a heavy-based flameproof casserole dish over medium heat. Season the shanks with salt and pepper, then add them to the dish and sear on all sides for 10 minutes or until golden brown.

Add the onion, carrot, celery, garlic, spices and herbs and cook, stirring frequently, for 5 minutes. Pour in the wine and stir to deglaze the dish. Bring the mixture to the boil, then add the tomatoes and stock or water, stirring to combine. Bring the mixture to the boil again and season with salt and pepper.

Cover the dish and transfer it to the oven. Reduce the temperature to 160°C (fan-forced) and cook for 2 hours or until the lamb is falling off the bone.

Meanwhile, to make the herbed couscous, scoop out 1 litre of the lamb cooking liquid in the dish. Place the couscous and olive oil in a large saucepan and stir to coat the grains. Set over medium heat and cook, stirring, for 1 minute, then pour in the lamb cooking liquid and stir. Bring to the boil and cook for 1 minute, then remove the pan from the heat and set aside, covered and stirring occasionally, for 30 minutes. Remove the lid and fluff up the couscous with a fork. Transfer to a bowl and stir through the lemon juice and herbs. Season well with salt and pepper and scatter over a few extra basil leaves.

Allow the lamb to rest in the dish for 30 minutes, then squeeze the garlic halves over the veg and stir through. Divide the lamb shanks and vegetables among plates and serve with the couscous on the side.

Lily & Maeve's Tip

This is the BEST couscous.

SLOW-COOKED BEEF CHEEK PLATE PIE

SERVES 4–6

Got a plate? Got a pie! This dish started life at my 4Fourteen restaurant, where it proved so popular that I soon began making it at home. It became the beef cheek 'plate pie' because we didn't have the right-sized pie dish, so I used a dinner plate instead. It turned out a treat! The pie filling doubles as a fantastic pasta sauce – simply shred the beef cheeks, combine with the veg and some leftover cooking liquid and toss through orecchiette.

2 beef cheeks, trimmed
plain flour, for dusting
sea salt and freshly ground
    black pepper
100 ml olive oil
2 onions, roughly chopped
2 carrots, roughly chopped
2 celery stalks, roughly chopped
1 garlic bulb, unpeeled, halved
    horizontally
2 bay leaves (fresh if possible)
½ bunch of thyme
½ bunch of marjoram
300 ml red wine
500 ml (2 cups) good-quality
    chicken stock
2 tablespoons dijon mustard
2 tablespoons worcestershire sauce
100 g (⅔ cup) frozen peas, thawed
bunch of cavolo nero, leaves and
    stalks finely chopped
1 sheet good-quality frozen puff
    pastry, just thawed
1 egg, beaten with a splash of
    full-cream milk
Celery Salad with Vierge Dressing
    (see page 16), to serve

Preheat the oven to 140°C (fan-forced).

Dust the beef cheeks in a little flour and season with salt and pepper. Heat the olive oil in a flameproof casserole dish over high heat. Add the seasoned beef cheeks and sear on all sides for 10 minutes or until brown and caramelised.

Add the onion, carrot, celery, garlic and herbs to the dish and cook, stirring, for 2 minutes. Pour in the wine and stir to deglaze the dish, then bring to the boil and add the chicken stock, mustard and worcestershire sauce. Bring to the boil again, then reduce the heat to a simmer and season with salt and pepper.

Put the lid on the dish, then transfer to the oven and cook for 3 hours or until the cheeks are completely soft.

Return the dish to the stovetop, squeeze the garlic halves over the beef and vegetables and stir through. Transfer the beef cheeks and vegetables to a separate dish (leaving the liquid behind) and stir the peas and cavolo nero through the hot beef and veg. Set the liquid over medium heat and cook for about 20 minutes or until the liquid has reduced by half. Season to taste with salt and pepper.

Increase the oven temperature to 160°C (fan-forced).

Transfer the beef cheeks and vegetables to a large deep dinner plate or pie dish and tear the beef cheeks into bite-sized pieces. Pour over the cooking liquid until it reaches the rim of the plate or dish and lay the puff-pastry sheet on top. Using your fingers, crimp the pastry to seal in the ingredients, then brush the egg wash over the top. Season the pastry with salt and pepper and poke a hole in the middle to allow steam to escape.

Transfer to the oven and cook for 40 minutes or until the pastry is lightly golden and the filling reaches 70°C on a kitchen thermometer.

Serve the pie with the celery salad.

BARBECUED LAMB LEG ON A BRICK WITH CHIMICHURRI

SERVES 6–8

Many of us have cooked a chook stuffed with a tinnie on the barbecue, so here's my barbecue hack for lamb, which takes things to the next level! You will need one clean household brick to make this dish, and you'll need to start the recipe the day before.

1 x 3 kg lamb leg, bone in
3 bunches of rosemary, leaves picked
    from 1 bunch
bunch of marjoram, leaves picked
20 pickled white anchovy fillets
10 garlic cloves, halved
olive oil, for brushing and drizzling
rock salt and freshly ground
    black pepper
juice of 2 lemons

CHIMICHURRI
½ small red onion, diced
3 garlic cloves, smashed
grated zest and juice of 1 lemon,
    plus extra if needed
3 thyme sprigs, leaves picked
handful of mint, leaves picked and
    roughly chopped
handful of flat-leaf parsley, leaves
    picked and roughly chopped
handful of coriander, leaves picked
    and roughly chopped
1 teaspoon finely chopped deseeded
    bird's eye chilli
½ teaspoon toasted and ground
    cumin seeds
150 ml extra-virgin olive oil

Using a small paring knife, slice 20 small incisions into the lamb to make 20 small pockets on the top and bottom of the leg. Stuff the pockets with the picked rosemary and marjoram leaves, anchovy fillets and garlic. Brush the lamb leg with olive oil and season with salt and pepper. Refrigerate, uncovered, overnight.

The next day, preheat a gas barbecue grill on high for 1 hour before you want to start cooking.

Meanwhile, grab a regular house brick and soak it in a bucket of cold water for 1 hour.

Place the brick in the middle of the barbecue grill and scatter the remaining rosemary bunches on top of the brick (this acts as a trivet, which keeps the lamb away from the hot grill and stops it from overcooking).

Place the studded lamb leg on top of the brick, then close the lid and leave for 10 minutes to come back up to temperature. Reduce the heat to low and cook the lamb for 20 minutes, then turn it over and cook for a further 20 minutes or until the lamb is caramelised all over with an internal temperature of 54°C on a kitchen thermometer.

Meanwhile, to make the chimichurri, place all the ingredients in a blender or the bowl of a food processor and blitz to a chunky or smooth sauce, depending on your preference. Taste and add a little extra lemon juice for acidity if you think the sauce needs it.

Remove the lamb from the barbecue and set aside to rest for 30 minutes. Season with salt and pepper and drizzle with olive oil and the lemon juice.

Carve the lamb and serve with the chimichurri on the side.

Any leftover chimichurri will keep in an airtight container in the fridge for up to 5 days.

CLASSIC ROAST RIB-EYE AND YORKSHIRE PUDS

SERVES 4

Follow my simple tips to create this show stopper of a dish for your next dinner party. It's a classic that never fails to impress. The trick to getting perfectly risen and crisp yorkies is to get the oil sizzling hot first and avoid opening the oven door during cooking!

sea salt and freshly ground
   black pepper
1 x 4 kg rack rib-eye of beef
2 onions, halved
2 garlic bulbs, unpeeled, halved
   horizontally
4 carrots
4 desiree potatoes, quartered
bunch of rosemary
bunch of thyme
100 ml vegetable oil
grated horseradish root,
   to serve (optional)
YORKSHIRE PUDDINGS
vegetable oil, for cooking
4 eggs
200 ml full-cream milk
40 g plain flour
sea salt and freshly ground
   black pepper

Preheat the oven to 220°C (fan-forced).

Heavily season the outside of the beef (this will ensure a beautiful crust once it is roasted).

To sear the beef you can either use a large heavy-based flameproof casserole dish or a barbecue flat plate. Heat either the dish over high heat or the barbecue to high, then add the beef and sear on all sides for 10–15 minutes, until well browned.

Place the onion, garlic, carrot and potato in a large roasting tin and lightly season, then position the herbs on top. Drizzle over the vegetable oil. Sit the seared beef on the herbs and roast in the oven for 10 minutes, then reduce the oven temperature to 160°C (fan-forced) and cook for 1½ hours or until the core temperature of the beef is 57°C on a kitchen thermometer. Remove the beef from the oven and allow to rest, covered, for at least 20 minutes.

Increase the oven temperature to 220°C (fan-forced).

Meanwhile, to make the Yorkshire puddings, pour enough vegetable oil to half-fill six holes of a large muffin tin, then place in the oven to heat up.

Whisk the eggs, milk and 1½ tablespoons of water in a large bowl, then rain in the flour and whisk vigorously to beat out the lumps. Season and set aside for 15 minutes, then pour the batter into a jug.

Very carefully remove the muffin tin from the oven and evenly pour the batter into the oiled muffin holes. Return to the oven and cook, undisturbed, for 20 minutes, until risen and golden.

Squeeze the garlic halves into the roasting tin and stir to mix through the vegetables.

Slice the beef, grate some horseradish over the top, if desired, and serve with the vegetables and Yorkshire puddings.

The Yorkshire puddings can be frozen once cooked and cooled. They will keep for up to 3 months. Simply reheat from frozen in a low oven.

SWEETS

RHUBARB JAM DOUGHNUTS

SERVES 8–10

These are my daughter Maeve's favourite.

25 g fresh yeast or 10 g instant
    dried yeast
35 g caster sugar, plus extra
    for rolling
100 ml full-cream milk
275 g plain flour, plus extra
    for dusting
1 teaspoon sea salt
2 eggs, plus 1 egg yolk
35 g unsalted butter, softened
vegetable oil, for deep-frying

RHUBARB JAM
1 kg rhubarb stalks, scrubbed
    clean and sliced
zest and juice of 2 oranges
750 g caster sugar
1 cinnamon stick
2 star anise
30 g pectin (see Tip)

Pectin can be purchased at most
health-food stores.

Place the yeast, sugar and milk in a bowl. Sit the bowl in another bowl of hot (not boiling) water and gently warm to 37°C to activate.

Meanwhile, to make the rhubarb jam, place the rhubarb, orange zest and juice, sugar, cinnamon stick, star anise and 500 ml (2 cups) of water in a large saucepan and bring to the boil over medium heat. Reduce the heat to a simmer and cook for 30 minutes or until the jam coats the back of a spoon without dripping. Stir through the pectin and add a little extra water until you reach your desired consistency. Set aside.

Place the yeast mixture, flour and salt in the bowl of a stand mixer with the dough hook attached and mix on low speed to combine. Add the eggs and egg yolk and mix again to incorporate. Add the butter and continue to mix for 5 minutes or until you have a smooth dough.

Transfer the dough to a large bowl dusted with flour and cover with plastic wrap. Set aside in a warm, dry place for 30 minutes or until the dough doubles in size.

Using floured hands, knead the dough back to its original size, then weigh out 20 g portions of dough and roll them into balls. Place the dough balls on a floured tray with space between them, to allow them to expand. Cover with a tea towel and set aside in a warm, dry place for 15–20 minutes until doubled in size again. Alternatively, if you are cooking the doughnuts later in the day, set aside in the fridge until needed.

Heat enough vegetable oil for deep-frying in a deep-fryer or large heavy-based saucepan to 170°C on a kitchen thermometer. Spread enough caster sugar to roll the doughnuts in on a large plate.

Working in batches, deep-fry the doughnuts, flipping regularly, for 3 minutes or until golden on all sides. Using a slotted spoon, transfer the doughnuts to a plate lined with paper towel to drain, then roll in the caster sugar.

Serve immediately with the rhubarb jam on the side for dipping.

Store the leftover jam in a jar in the fridge for up to 3 months.

MIXED BERRY POPSICLES

MAKES 6-8

These popsicles are a cheap and easy way to make a healthy dessert for the family. As there are so few ingredients, I recommend using a good-quality plain yoghurt. You'll need a popsicle mould and popsicle sticks to make this recipe.

500 g (2 cups) plain yoghurt
1 tablespoon glucose syrup
1 teaspoon citric acid
200 g frozen mixed berries
250 g dark chocolate (70% cocoa
  solids), broken into squares
  (optional)

Place the yoghurt, glucose and citric acid in a saucepan over low heat. Stir until the glucose has melted, then pour the mixture into a bowl set over an ice bath and stir in the berries. Keep stirring until the mixture is completely cool.

Gently pour the mixture into six to eight popsicle moulds and place in the freezer for 1 hour. Remove the moulds and insert a popsicle stick into the base of each popsicle, then return the mould to the freezer for at least 6 hours, but preferably overnight, until completely set.

If using, place the chocolate in a bowl set over a saucepan of simmering water and stir until melted. Set aside to cool slightly.

To serve, run the outside of the moulds under warm water, then twist to release the popsicles. Dip into the melted chocolate, if using, and allow to set slightly, then serve straight away.

CHOCOLATE-ORANGE MOUSSE WITH HOMEMADE HONEYCOMB

SERVES 4

Everyone needs a good chocolate dessert in their repertoire and this is mine. Honeycomb is easy to make at home and I encourage you to give it a go; just keep any leftovers in the freezer to stop it going soft.

200 g dark chocolate (70% cocoa
    solids), plus extra, grated, to serve
90 ml double cream
3 tablespoons caster sugar
zest and juice of 2 oranges
4 egg whites
HONEYCOMB
480 g caster sugar
75 g honey
185 g glucose syrup
25 g bicarbonate of soda

Place the chocolate, double cream and sugar in a bowl set over a saucepan of simmering water. Stir until the chocolate has melted, then stir through orange zest and juice. Leave to infuse for 1 hour, then strain to remove the zest. Transfer the chocolate mixture to a bowl and set aside in the fridge.

Using electric beaters or a stand mixer with the whisk attached, beat the egg whites until stiff peaks form. Fold through the chocolate mixture, then return to the fridge for 2 hours or until set.

Meanwhile, to make the honeycomb, line a large baking tray with baking paper.

Place the sugar, honey, glucose and 90 ml of water in a deep saucepan over high heat. Without stirring, heat the mixture to 145°C on a kitchen thermometer, then sift in the bicarbonate of soda and whisk quickly and thoroughly to combine – the mixture will foam up and increase in size. Quickly pour the honeycomb mixture onto the prepared tray and lightly spread it out to a 5 cm-thick even layer. Set aside to cool.

Divide the chocolate–orange mousse among serving bowls. Break the cooled honeycomb into shards and use some of them to decorate the top of each mousse. Grate over a little extra chocolate and serve.

Any leftover honeycomb will keep in an airtight container in the freezer for up to 1 week.

BAKED VERBENA PLUMS

SERVES 8

The beauty of this dish is its flexibility. I love the tartness of baked plums, but they can be easily swapped for apricots, peaches or nectarines, or any other stone fruit that is in abundance. This dish tastes even better served cold the next day.

20 small plums
300 ml dessert wine
20 lemon verbena leaves
   (lemon thyme also works well)
2 fresh bay leaves
2½ tablespoons golden syrup
1 lemon, halved
Marmalade and Toast Ice Cream
   (see page 214), to serve

Preheat the oven to 200°C (fan-forced).

Place the plums and dessert wine in a large baking or casserole dish.

Crush or tear the verbena leaves and bay leaves in your hands, then toss them through the plums and wine. Add the golden syrup and toss again, then transfer to the oven and bake for about 30 minutes, until the fruit is mushy and the cooking liquid is thick and syrupy.

Divide the plums among bowls and squeeze over the lemon halves. Spoon over the delicious syrup and serve with marmalade and toast ice cream on the side.

ETON MESS

SERVES 4

This looks like a very simple dish, but it's full of different flavours and textures. You can change up the fruit according to the season. It's a great way to use up leftover egg whites, too.

300 g strawberries, hulled
  and quartered
¼ teaspoon sea salt
1 teaspoon caster sugar
juice of ½ lemon
mint leaves, to serve (optional)

ITALIAN MERINGUE
185 g caster sugar
185 g glucose syrup
3 large egg whites

WHIPPED CREAM
225 ml double cream
1 teaspoon icing sugar
½ teaspoon vanilla essence

To make the Italian meringue, combine the caster sugar, glucose and 100 ml of water in a small saucepan and bring to 118°C.

Meanwhile, place the egg whites in the bowl of a stand mixer with the whisk attached. Beat on medium speed until soft peaks form. Once the sugar mixture has reached 118°C, slowly pour it into the egg white in a thin continuous stream, then whisk on high speed for 15 minutes. Rest for 3 hours (or overnight for a crispier result).

Preheat the oven to 100°C (fan-forced). Line a baking tray with baking paper.

Spread the meringue over the prepared baking tray to a thickness of 5 mm and bake for 1 hour. If it is still too soft or chewy, reduce the oven temperature by 10°C and cook until crisp. Turn the oven off, then leave the meringue inside the oven to completely cool. Once cool, break the meringue into shards.

Meanwhile, place the strawberries, salt, sugar and lemon juice in a large mixing bowl and toss to combine. Set aside for 30–40 minutes, until the strawberries are soft and macerated.

To make the whipped cream, clean the bowl of the stand mixer, then place all the ingredients in the bowl and whisk on medium speed until you have light peaks. Set aside.

To assemble, place a few macerated strawberries and their juice in sundae glasses or serving bowls. Top with a layer of meringue shards and a generous dessertspoon of cream. Repeat the layering until you've used all the ingredients, top with some mint leaves if you like, then serve immediately.

PEACH TARTE TATIN

SERVES 4–6

I like to use yellow peaches in this tarte tatin because they hold up well during cooking, but apples and pears work equally well. It's also delicious with ripe pineapple when it's in season.

130 g caster sugar
1 vanilla bean, split and seeds
    scraped, or 1 teaspoon vanilla
    bean paste
1 cinnamon stick
2 star anise
110 g salted butter
6 yellow peaches, halved,
    stones removed
1 sheet good-quality frozen
    puff pastry, just thawed
1 egg, lightly beaten
ice cream (see page 214), to serve

Preheat the oven to 190°C fan-forced.

Place the sugar, vanilla seeds, cinnamon, star anise and 2½ tablespoons of water in a large ovenproof frying pan over medium heat. Cook, without stirring, until the sugar dissolves and turns a light amber colour, then remove the cinnamon and star anise (or leave in to serve, then remove) and continue to cook the sugar until it reaches a dark bourbon caramel. Stir through the butter until melted, then set aside to cool until hard.

Place the peach halves, cut-side down, in the pan and cover with the puff pastry, tucking in the edges around the peach halves. Brush the pastry with the beaten egg and bake for 20 minutes or until the pastry is puffed up and golden brown.

Allow the tarte tatin to rest for 10 minutes, then gently press and slowly twist the pastry to release the sticky peach on the base. Place a serving plate on top and quickly flip the tarte tatin onto the plate.

Cut into thick slices and serve with ice cream.

Simple but impressive. Change up the fruit according to the season or what you have on hand.

GINGER AND CINNAMON CRÈME CARAMEL

SERVES 4–6

This is my version of a crème caramel. The ginger and cinnamon add a lovely warmth to this luscious and indulgent dessert. It's creamy and crisp all at the same time. It really brings back memories of the sweets trolley as a kid. You will need to start this recipe the day before.

330 g caster sugar
500 ml (2 cups) pouring cream
375 ml (1½ cups) full-cream milk
2 cinnamon sticks
10 g ginger, finely grated
1 tablespoon vanilla essence
6 whole eggs plus 2 egg yolks,
    lightly beaten

Place one-third of the sugar and 125 ml (½ cup) of water in a very clean saucepan over medium heat. Bring to the boil and cook, without stirring, for 6–8 minutes, until a caramel starts to form. Carefully pour the caramel into a 20 cm-diameter pie or baking dish and set aside to cool.

Preheat the oven to 140°C (fan-forced).

Place the cream, milk, cinnamon, ginger and vanilla in a saucepan and bring to a simmer over medium heat – do not let the mixture boil. Remove from the heat and set aside.

Place the beaten egg and remaining sugar in a large mixing bowl, then slowly pour in the milk and cream mixture, whisking constantly, until you have a smooth custard. Carefully strain the custard into the dish over the caramel.

Lay a tea towel in the base of a large deep roasting tin and place the pie or baking dish on top – this prevents the crème caramel from overcooking. Pour enough water into the roasting tin to come halfway up the side of the dish. Tightly cover with foil before putting it in the oven, to prevent it from caramelising.

Bake for 1 hour or until the custard is set around the edges with a slight wobble in the middle. Set aside to cool, then place in the fridge overnight to chill and completely set.

The next day, run a small, sharp knife around the crème caramel, place a serving plate on top of the dish and carefully invert the caramel onto the plate and serve.

DATE PUDDING WITH DULCE DE LECHE

SERVES 6

I like to make more dulce de leche than I need for this recipe, as it keeps indefinitely if left unopened in the can. Serve it with ice cream, spread it on toast or eat directly from the can with a spoon.

150 ml dark rum
1 vanilla bean, split and seeds scraped
250 g dates, pitted
125 g salted butter, softened,
    plus extra for greasing
100 g caster sugar
3 eggs, beaten
250 g (1⅔ cups) plain flour
2 teaspoons bicarbonate of soda
whipped cream, to serve
DULCE DE LECHE
2 x 395 ml cans condensed milk

To make the dulce de leche, place the unopened cans in a large saucepan and add enough cold water to cover the cans by three times their height. It is really important that the cans remain submerged in plenty of water during cooking; otherwise they may explode.

Bring the water to the boil, then reduce the heat to a low simmer and cook for 3–4 hours, topping up with more water if needed. The longer you simmer the cans, the thicker your dulce de leche will be.

Remove the pan from the heat and allow the cans to cool to room temperature in the pan before opening.

Place the rum, vanilla seeds and 250 ml (1 cup) of water in a saucepan and bring to the boil over medium heat. Add the dates, then remove the pan from the heat and set aside for 1 hour to allow the dates to plump up and absorb the liquid.

Blitz half the date mixture using a hand-held blender and roughly chop the remaining mixture to retain some texture.

Preheat the oven to 180°C (fan-forced).

Meanwhile, using electric beaters or in the bowl of a stand mixer with the whisk attached, beat the butter and sugar until fluffy and pale. Slowly pour in the beaten egg in a thin, steady stream, whisking constantly, until completely combined. Reduce the speed to low, then add the flour and bicarbonate of soda and mix to completely combine. Swap to a metal spoon and fold in the blitzed and chopped date mixture.

Grease a baking dish with butter. Pour the date batter into the dish, then place the dish in a large deep roasting tin. Pour enough boiling water into the tin to come halfway up the side of the baking dish, then transfer to the oven and bake for 20–25 minutes, until a skewer inserted into the pudding comes out clean.

Remove the baking dish from the tin and allow the pudding to cool. Open one of the cans of dulce de leche.

Divide the pudding among serving plates, spoon the warm dulce de leche over the top and serve with whipped cream.

FRUITY CLAFOUTIS

SERVES 6–8

A classic French dessert that's incredibly simple to make. Clafoutis is traditionally made with cherries, but any in-season stone fruit works well.

50 g almonds
1 tablespoon strong flour
100 g caster sugar
2 whole eggs plus 3 egg yolks
250 ml (1 cup) pouring cream
1 vanilla bean, split and seeds scraped
100 g frozen pitted cherries, thawed
100 g peaches, stones removed,
  cut into wedges
100 g strawberries, hulled and halved
  or quartered if large
icing sugar, for dusting

Place the almonds, flour and caster sugar in the bowl of a food processor and blend for 2 minutes. Add the whole eggs and egg yolks, cream and vanilla seeds and blend until smooth. Transfer the mixture to a bowl and set aside in the fridge to rest for at least 6 hours.

Preheat the oven to 190°C (fan-forced).

Place the fruit in the bottom of a baking dish or cast-iron frying pan. Pour the chilled batter over the fruit and bake for 10 minutes or until the batter is set and golden brown on top.

Dust with icing sugar and serve.

ELDERFLOWER JELLY WITH BLACKBERRIES

SERVES 6

For me, this dessert is summer in a bowl.

375 g blackberries (see Tips)
½ teaspoon sea salt
1 tablespoon caster sugar
zest and juice of 1 lemon
ELDERFLOWER JELLY
100 g brown sugar
½ vanilla bean, split and seeds scraped
7 lemon verbena leaves (see Tips)
12 elderflower heads (see Tips)
4 titanium-strength gelatine leaves
juice of 2 lemons

To make the elderflower jelly, place the brown sugar, vanilla seeds and 1 litre of water in a saucepan over medium heat. Bring to the boil, then scrunch the lemon verbena leaves in your hands until they release their aroma and add them to the water. Remove the pan from the heat, stir through the elderflower heads and set aside to steep.

Meanwhile, place the gelatine leaves in a bowl of cold water and set aside for a minute or two until soft.

Remove the gelatine leaves from the bowl, shake off any excess water and add them to the warm elderflower liquid. Stir through the lemon juice and set aside until the gelatine is completely dissolved. Pour the mixture into a large serving bowl or individual serving glasses (strain it if you prefer), then place in the fridge for at least 6 hours until set.

About 30 minutes before you want to serve the dessert, place the blackberries in a bowl, toss through the salt, caster sugar and lemon zest and juice, and set aside to macerate until the blackberries start to release their juice.

Spoon the macerated blackberries and their juice over the elderflower jelly, then take to the table and serve.

TIPS

You can replace the blackberries with any in-season berries.

If elderflower heads are tricky to come by, substitute 300 ml of elderflower cordial instead.

You can also use one bunches of mint leaves instead of the lemon verbena leaves.

BRIOCHE AND BUTTER PUDDING

SERVES 8–10

This is a rich and decadent version of traditional bread and butter pudding that's almost as good as my mate Matt Kemp's. Almost ... You will need to start this recipe the day before.

250 g raisins
200 ml port, Pedro Ximénez
   or your favourite rum
8 egg yolks
400 ml pouring cream
300 ml full-cream milk
60 g glucose syrup
150 g caster sugar
salted butter, for spreading
2 x 350 g day-old brioche loaves,
   thickly sliced
1 tablespoon ground cinnamon
1 tablespoon freshly grated nutmeg

Soak the raisins in the alcohol for a minimum of 6 hours but preferably overnight to soak up all the liquid.

The next day, whisk the egg yolks in a large mixing bowl until light and fluffy.

Place the cream, milk, glucose and 50 g of sugar in a saucepan and bring to the boil.

Whisking constantly, very slowly pour the hot cream and milk mixture over the egg yolks in a thin, steady stream. Whisk until completely combined, then pour the mixture back into the saucepan and slowly warm over low heat until the mixture reaches 80°C on a kitchen thermometer.

Meanwhile, fill a large bowl with ice and place another large bowl on top to chill. Pour the custard into the chilled bowl and stir continuously until cold.

Butter the brioche slices on one side, then layer half the brioche in a large baking dish so the slices are overlapping and scatter over half the boozy raisins. Pour half the custard over brioche, then repeat with another layer of brioche, raisins and custard. Cover the dish with plastic wrap, then place a tray on top and weigh it down with a few cans. Set aside in the fridge for 6 hours.

Preheat the oven to 180°C (fan-forced). Place a clean tea towel in the bottom of a large roasting tin that will fit your baking dish.

Combine the cinnamon, nutmeg and remaining sugar in a small bowl, then sprinkle the mixture over the brioche.

Place the dish in the prepared roasting tin and pour enough warm water into the tin to come halfway up the side of the baking dish. Bake for 35–40 minutes, until the pudding is golden on top and the custard is just set with a slight wobble.

Serve warm.

THE PERFECT ICE-CREAM BASE FOR MANY FLAVOURS (OR CHOOSE YOUR OWN ADVENTURE ICE CREAM!)

MAKES 1.5 LITRES

Don't be afraid to make your own ice cream at home. It's so easy I think everyone should have a go. This recipe is a great base for many flavours. I have included the three most popular in our house: jam; marmalade and toast; and chocolate and hazelnut. Once you have mastered the basics, you'll have your very own ice-cream shop at your fingertips. You will need to start this recipe the day before.

16 egg yolks (save the egg whites to make meringues or my Eton Mess on page 201!)
600 ml pouring cream
600 ml full-cream milk
100 g caster sugar
120 g glucose syrup

Whisk the egg yolks in a large mixing bowl until light and fluffy.

Place the cream, milk, sugar and glucose in a saucepan and bring to the boil.

Whisking constantly, very slowly pour the hot cream and milk mixture over the egg yolks in a thin, steady stream. Whisk until completely combined, then pour the mixture back into the saucepan and slowly warm over low heat until the mixture reaches 84°C on a kitchen thermometer.

Meanwhile, fill a large bowl with ice and place another large bowl on top to chill.

Pour the custard into the chilled bowl and stir continuously until cold. Cover and set aside in the fridge overnight. The next day, pour the custard into an ice-cream machine, along with your chosen flavour (see below for ideas or add your own). Churn according to the manufacturer's instructions, then transfer to an airtight container and place in the freezer overnight to completely set.

The ice cream will keep in the freezer for 2–3 weeks.

HERE ARE SOME OF MY FAVOURITE ICE-CREAM FLAVOURS

RASPBERRY OR STRAWBERRY JAM
Swirl 330 g raspberry or strawberry jam through the ice-cream base.

MARMALADE AND TOAST
Add 330 g marmalade to the ice-cream base and stir to completely combine. Blitz two slices of warm toast in the bowl of a food processor and stir through.

CHOCOLATE AND HAZELNUT
Swirl 330 g of chocolate hazelnut spread through the ice-cream base.

MARMALADE AND TOAST

CHOCOLATE AND HAZELNUT

RASPBERRY OR STRAWBERRY JAM

CONVERSION CHARTS

Measuring cups and spoons may vary slightly from one country to another, but the difference is generally not enough to affect a recipe. All cup and spoon measures are level.

One Australian metric measuring cup holds 250 ml (8 fl oz), one Australian tablespoon holds 20 ml (4 teaspoons) and one Australian metric teaspoon holds 5 ml. North America, New Zealand and the UK use a 15 ml (3-teaspoon) tablespoon.

LENGTH

METRIC	IMPERIAL
3 mm	⅛ inch
6 mm	¼ inch
1 cm	½ inch
2.5 cm	1 inch
5 cm	2 inches
18 cm	7 inches
20 cm	8 inches
23 cm	9 inches
25 cm	10 inches
30 cm	12 inches

LIQUID MEASURES

ONE AMERICAN PINT	ONE IMPERIAL PINT
500 ml (16 fl oz)	600 ml (20 fl oz)

CUP	METRIC	IMPERIAL
⅛ cup	30 ml	1 fl oz
¼ cup	60 ml	2 fl oz
⅓ cup	80 ml	2½ fl oz
½ cup	125 ml	4 fl oz
⅔ cup	160 ml	5 fl oz
¾ cup	180 ml	6 fl oz
1 cup	250 ml	8 fl oz
2 cups	500 ml	16 fl oz
2¼ cups	560 ml	20 fl oz
4 cups	1 litre	32 fl oz

DRY MEASURES

The most accurate way to measure dry ingredients is to weigh them. However, if using a cup, add the ingredient loosely to the cup and level with a knife; don't compact the ingredient unless the recipe requests 'firmly packed'.

METRIC	IMPERIAL
15 g	½ oz
30 g	1 oz
60 g	2 oz
125 g	4 oz (¼ lb)
185 g	6 oz
250 g	8 oz (½ lb)
375 g	12 oz (¾ lb)
500 g	16 oz (1 lb)
1 kg	32 oz (2 lb)

OVEN TEMPERATURES

CELSIUS	FAHRENHEIT	CELSIUS	GAS MARK
100°C	200°F	110°C	¼
120°C	250°F	130°C	½
150°C	300°F	140°C	1
160°C	325°F	150°C	2
180°C	350°F	170°C	3
200°C	400°F	180°C	4
220°C	425°F	190°C	5
		200°C	6
		220°C	7
		230°C	8
		240°C	9
		250°C	10

THANKS

Mary Small, credit for working out my recipe wall.

Lucy Heaver and Clare Marshall, for the editing.

Sharon Timms, for all your help with the introduction – you saved my sanity.

Kirby Armstrong, for the beautiful design.

Alan Benson (we ride again).

Emma Knowles (great stories).

Peta Dent ('I'll just pop to the shops.')

Jimmy Callaway, my food son – 10 years, still strong.

Sara Eastwood, keep doing what you do xx

To all who have eaten in my house, this book is in part yours.

My family in Ireland, both north and south, my love for this type of food was born with you.

To my business partners, Clayton, Darren and Jane, for putting up with me.

Marlon Dalton, for his cheese and the red wine.

Ronni Kahn at OzHarvest, you have given me passion for food and life.

Thanks to my suppliers: Will Brunker at Joto Fresh Fish; Anthony and Rebecca Puharich and family at Vic's Meats; Isaac Piper and family at Cloudy Bay Clams; Alex Olsson at Olsson's Salt; Katrina and Sam Sparke at Redleaf Farm for their pork; Mitch and Kylie at Australian Pork (where would I be without you?); the Maroubra mafia at Pacific Square (Peters Meats, Deli Hub and Billy's Bar Espresso); and the Sydney Fish Market.

Thanks to all our loyal staff at Terminus Pyrmont and Banksia Bistro, who are serving this food to people every day.

Thanks to my second lot of kids – Danielle, Adam and Vanessa – who critiqued EVERY dish I made. Let's just leave it at that!

To my dogs, Ellie and Brann, who know more about me than anyone else. I enjoy our D & Ms.

And finally, last but certainly not least, thank you to Jane, Lily and Maeve. I've said this before, but thank you again for putting up with me.

Jane, I couldn't have done this without you, Bub xx

Lily, so sensitive and caring, I love your baking skills xx

Maeve, I know one day I will be working for you xx

- Belly Sausage Roll/chicken terrine.
- Raw Fish Ginger Vin.
- Coli, miso, mussels
- ~~XO Scotch Egg~~
- Steak + kidney — on Toast
- Pea, Labneh, mint, melon - Toast
- pickled mussels
- Escaseche — "Fish Recipe"
- Tomato Bread "Spam"
- Liver Jaffrel
- Stuffed pumpkin x 2 ways
- Coli cheese + Greece → Soup
- Barly Rizo
- Roast orange carrots Rendale
- Lamb BBQ Ribs
- Cured Salmon - trout.
- Smoked mackrel/kipper
- "Dashi Jelly" - Tuna-seaweed

- Pea/Broad Beens — Bran
  Salt Fish — Soup?
  chicken liver — isreal
- Pizzia (Quick Bread) Mushroom
  in raw
- Cured — Seared — Trout
  — "kilie"
- Asian eggs — Green sc
- Tomato Ice pops —
- chicken parmasan Rind — Soup
  — kidney Rosemary Sticks.
- Bisque —
  — "prawn cocktail"
  "Spring Veg Soup"
  Tomato —

S A l t s :
                        (pische)
— Basic Tom Sa
— Thousnge Roll "??
— Green Sc. "Was
— Sambal?

olive Green Sc.
Rwberts vin dressing

oysters Vietnemese ✓
smoked salmon terrine ✓

Fennel salad (@ watermelen/ Mums "Rice Salad"
Smoked Eel - Soup?? (+ feta) Donappx salad

INDEX

Duck Confit + Lentil

MEAT LOAF /Nut.

- Bone marrow "toast"
- Ox tail-cheek② Dumpling

- GINGER Soy chicken ① (packed) - Pork fillet.

/ BBQ Brick

- BAD BOYS + Chic Bread

Stuffed Cabbage. -

- BEEF PLATE Pie. Maeve is so amazing

CRumbel - Fish

Weed / Green / Riddle Pie

- HAM Hock / Baked w. Beans
- LIVER — onions
Lamb "Timmy" Baked potato
"king" + pickle

- Baked fish / Toms / Fennel / Persian / Clam..

- Chic Snit — Out CRumbel Batter-Roll.
- Fried fish — Sambal 2

mushroom, lentil, miso stew.
LAMB LEG (BBQ ON A Bench)

- LAMB BOLL X — Braise Roast Confit. Gratin.

"IRISH Stew" 2020."
2 Rolled Lamb — "Bonfire"

- LAMB - Root Pie

CRumbel Pork Cutlet

- Roast Skate Brown Butter

Lamb - Potatoes "Spiced"

- Clams Sorrel — Fried Bread
Confit Chic - maryland Harisse
- Beef cheek
Corned Beef tatties

• Pies

Green + chees

- Salt Baked chicken

- Fish Pie

- Roast Hock — pea salad

- Steak kidney

- Next DAY Stew veg

H2 — mince
— Bolognese 3 Meats

Bad girls - Chicken Wings

- Whole Dory - Seaweed butter

Maeve is so amazing

- Whole Pork Belly - Roast.
- Pork Neck

- Tom fish Stew

- Mussels —   / — Clam Stew —

. 1 Doughnut Triffle — ② ⑥? ① Doughnuts + cheese

④ Rice pudding   ② Sandwich Iceberg   ⑤ Lemon - V.
                                          + fand pollen
- pineapple - Verbeana salt - Lime syrup.   Lily is
         "MX MAGNUM"   Cheese Bread — "posh"   Amazing.
- choc mouss,   MALT ICe . + BALIC
                                              ↑ Sweet
— Apricots + Roast Poached H — Lemon Curd - 2 Savory
                    pudding   — MY choc ICE rev
— plum tart + Roast — Yogh   — Bread — —   (Kempx
                              — Eton mess - Goosed
    → Ice Cream churned   — Pops . / Sw, 35 Roll
      + Rice pudding   — Summer pudding Ice
         Coln style
         § Amazing/   — Tort . try tom -
         terreble   (thorton) (Quince
                              — Clafoutis - cherry
Sausage "Bushe.   — Frozen Delice — Nut.
Meat Balls — "Herb"   — Licorice parent.
— Blue mackerel + Rubeds   — Jelly Overflow +tip
— Spanish mackerel - Cutlet   — "macerated fruit.
— Grilled flounder - prawn butter — "Micro" [merangue]
— Veal Snff (whole)   poached [Island.   ]
      + singel!   — Berries - Sabyen. (1441
  dk Porchetta + Green   — Sweet Jaffad.
  Cafe with Sandwich +pread!!
                              — MY toffee "Dolce Car"
Lily   — syrups -
is   — Coffee — Di - Bella ???
Not   — Pressd
Amazing   madadllas | Kettl
               cheese
               piecrust.

A Plum book
First published in 2020 by
Pan Macmillan Australia Pty Limited
Level 25, 1 Market Street,
Sydney, NSW 2000, Australia

Level 3, 112 Wellington Parade,
East Melbourne, VIC 3002, Australia

Design by Kirby Armstrong
Edited by Lucy Heaver
Index by Helena Holmgren
Photography by Alan Benson
Food and prop styling by Emma Knowles
Food preparation by James Callaway, Peta Dent and Colin Fassnidge
Typeset by Kirby Armstrong
Colour reproduction by Splitting Image Colour Studio
Printed and bound in China by 1010 Printing International Limited

A CIP catalogue record for this book is available from the National Library of Australia.

10 9 8 7 6 5 4 3 2 1